AVICENNA
CUISINE

Your Personalized Guidebook
on Balanced Eating and Living

SAMIRA ARDALAN

INTRODUCTION BY
LALEH BAKHTIAR

AVICENNA TIME

Library of Congress Cataloging-in-Publication Data
Avicenna™Cuisine—a Guidebook
1. Cooking. 2. History of Foods. 3. Special Diet I. Title.

ISBN 13: 978-1567444100
ISBN 10: 1567444105

Cover Design and Illustrations by Samira Ardalan unless otherwise indicated.

Logo Design: Haleh Hashemi
Back Cover Headshot: Ken Rochon

Published by
Avicenna Time

Distributed by
KAZI Publications, Inc.
3023 W. Belmont Avenue Chicago IL 60618
Tel: 773-267-7001; FAX: 773-267-7002
email: info@kazi.org
www.kazi.org

CONTENTS

LIST OF ILLUSTRATIONS

PREFACE

HELLO, MY NAME IS SAMIRA ARDALAN. I was born on July 26th, 1989 in Albuquerque, New Mexico. I'm a Leo and fiery lioness at heart. When I was young I was never afraid to speak my mind. My family and friends used to tell me I was a firecracker and always full of spunk and energy. I played varsity soccer at Severna Park High School in Maryland and love reminiscing on those sweet goals, the sound of the ball striking my cleat, and the crowd jumping up and down in excitement. This was all I knew, until one day at a very young age, I was lucky enough to discover my passion.

After soccer practice and team dinners, I would come home and watch Food Network and that was pretty much it. Nothing else was as interesting. My favorites, in no particular order, are Good Eats with Alton Brown, Boy Meets Grill with Bobby Flay, Molto Mario, Tyler's Ultimate, Every Italian with Giada De Laurentiis and Barefoot Contessa with Ina Garten.

Other entertaining shows were Top Chef and Iron Chef and in 2006 when I saw the first episode of Top Chef, I started telling my family I wanted to try out. I never did, but hey, there is still plenty of time! In the meantime, at the age of 16, and in search of my first job, I knew it had to involve food and, if I got lucky at my young age, I would get to cook too.

I remember researching online for restaurants and catering companies in my hometown. I was fortunate to find a catering company close by that was fairly new. I will never forget the first day I walked in to apply. I saw one of my classmates in the kitchen cutting Romaine Lettuce and de-seeding Roma Tomatoes for Pico de Gallo. Why was this exciting to me? All I can say is that at that moment I wished I were her, having my own cutting board, using that knife, learning new techniques, and mastering a recipe from beginning to end, tasting and munching along the way.

Two years later, I found myself having a complete understanding of many cooking techniques, preparations, flavor combinations in addition to high-end service and the hospitality industry from all the events we catered. I want to thank Kerri Rowe from Kerri Out Foods for giving me that opportunity and teaching me so much. It was an experience of a lifetime. Having learned to cook with such fresh, healthy ingredients, spices, and herbs gave me confidence in the kitchen. At this point, I was able to watch a Food Network episode and not just re-create the dish from the top of my head, but was also able to incorporate my own creative twists to the dish. My mom, step-dad and brothers can tell you they were spoiled rotten for a few years there, and I certainly enjoyed cooking family dinners on the reg!

When it was time for college, I decided to study Business Management at Towson University. I knew one day I wanted to start my own company, so this was a perfect fit. Five years later I was thrilled to be hired as the Marketing Manager at a beautiful boutique hotel called Capella Washington, D.C., Georgetown. I was one of the first team members on board for this new property and I grew tremendously during those two years. I was fortunate enough to write an insider food and recipe blog based on new menu items and holiday offerings that the hotel and restaurant Chefs were working on throughout the seasons. Tasting the dishes and also photographing them made the job feel like a hobby.

My favorite dining experience was when we were going through a soft opening of the restaurant and I was unexpectedly served a 48 oz. Cote Boeuf served and sliced tableside. The best part of the meal was that I got to share this bone-in rib steak with the CEO & Founder of Capella Hotels, Horst Schulze. I'll never forget that legacy moment.

One day on my commute home to Maryland, I called my grandmother, Laleh Bakhtiar, who lives in Chicago, just as I always did on my way home. I asked her what she was working on. Typically her responses were extremely interesting, given that she has 147 titles on Amazon, mainly various aspects of Islamic Civilization and Culture. She happened to be working on the English translation of Avicenna's (also known as Ibn Sina), Canon of Medicine. The Canon of Medicine is an encyclopedia of medicine in five books compiled by this famous Persian philosopher and physician of the 11th Century CE. Encyclopedia Britannica has called it the single most important book in the history of medicine.

So I wondered, who was Avicenna? Turns out he was known as the Father of Modern Medicine and the Prince of Physicians. Avicenna's tested system for natural healing was used in Europe for over 600 years. By the age of 21, Avicenna turned to medicine and began his prodigious writing career. His 240 books cross numerous fields, including mathematics, geometry, astronomy, physics, metaphysics, philology, music, and poetry. While basing his medical system on the humoral and vitalistic concepts of two other outstanding figures in the history of medicine, Hippocrates and Galen, Avicenna's writing in the Canon took a universal perspective, collecting, distilling and synthesizing all the medical knowledge that existed at his time, including different medical systems from India (Aryuvedic),

Chinese, Greek (Unani), Persian, Egyptian, Hindu and Tibetan.

When my grandmother began to tell me about Volume 2, Natural Pharmaceuticals, I was extremely intrigued. Volume 2 holds a treasure of information on what was known as the simple natural pharmaceuticals used for over 1,000 years to heal various diseases and disorders. Avicenna includes the individual plants, herbs, animals and minerals that have healing properties in addition to tested formulas and natural medications. On our second and third call, my grandmother would ask me things such as: Did you know research has shown that Saffron has anti-oxidant, anti-depressant, and anti-cancer properties? Or that Turmeric is used for arthritis, heartburn, stomach pain, headaches, kidney problems and even infected wounds?

My interest grew so quickly that I wanted a copy for myself to better understand and research. I discovered that the basis of our health explained in the *Canon* resulting in our Temperament revolves around our four humors. It was fascinating learning about the humours: blood (sanguine humor, hot and wet), yellow bile (choleric humor, hot and dry), phlegm (phlegmatic humor, cold and wet) and black bile (atrabilious humor, cold and dry) and that in all other living things, Temperament is formed from the four classical elements of air, fire, water and earth that have the same hot, cold, wet, dry combinations of qualities. These seem to correlate to the four states of matter: gas (air, hot and wet), plasma (fire, hot and dry), liquid (water, cold and wet) and solid (earth, cold and dry). So although this book is from the 11th century, it still is very relevant and makes total sense that our health would depend on the balance of these four elements of life.

A few weeks and conversations later, I had a shining Aha moment. I thought to myself, what if Avicenna's tested medical system of natural healing and balance of the body, mind and energy was transformed into a food concept? What if I could abridge and adapt his holistic approach of medicine into a modern Cuisine where we eat and live healthy according to our body's unique make up?

My grandma, Laleh told me that the first step to understanding my body and becoming my own doctor is getting to know myself through a Temperament Test. You can take yours here in this book (page 165) or on our website at avicennacuisine.com. My results came back that I am primarily Airy, or Sanguine and secondarily Fiery, or Choleric. It is possible to have just one Temperament, or have a secondary as well. The strengths of my Temperament are that I am: extroverted, people-oriented, enthusiastic, resolute, organized and productive. My weaknesses are: opinionated, easily angered, forgetful, stubborn, justify my actions and tend to be obnoxious if threatened. I have a Temperamental quality between Air and Fire. This means that I have an overall dominant quality of heat in my body, since Air is hot and wet and Fire is hot and dry. Any change in the ideal level of heat, especially an increase in heat will negatively affect me. My appetite is "The Epicure." I have cravings for rich gourmet foods that are typically quite hearty. Because of my secondary Fiery Temperament, I also am fond of fried, spicy and salty foods with intense taste sensations.

One of my favorite parts about this book is when you discover your Temperament and afterwards go to the Temperament Chapter (page 75) to discover more about your personality, appetite, digestion, and how to create optimum health in your body, mind and energy through Avicenna's 6 Nurturing Essentials: Air & Environment, Physical Rest & Activity, Sleep & Wakefulness, Emotions & Aromatherapy, Retention & Evacuation, and last but not least, Food, Diet & Drink.

For example, since I have a dominance of heat in my body, it is best for me to eat primarily cold and dry-tempered foods (the opposite of hot and wet) to maintain balance. Cold tempered meats and fish for instance are salmon, chicken and shrimp. Dry-tempered vegetables include peppers, garlic, onions and cauliflower and dry-tempered fruits include grapefruit and olives. It is best for me to eat cold tempered spices and herbs as well such as cilantro, mint and parsley to maintain balance.

The Avicenna Cuisine Guidebook does not give you recipes for each Temperament result just yet. This book gives you a look at the ingredients you should be cooking with, in addition to the other 6 Nurturing Essentials I mentioned above. My goal with this book is to provide you with answers, based on Avicenna Cuisine, to help you better understand your body's reactions to foods and how they create balances or imbalances in your body. If you determine that you are in fact in a balanced state, with no health problems or digestive problems with the foods you eat, then we can say that you can continue eating, living, and exercising the way you do.

If you feel out of balance, maybe more fatigued or depressed than normal, we need to re-evaluate what you are eating and how you are living on a day-to-day basis. Maintaining balance creates good health and depends on eating the right tempered foods for your particular Temperament. Recipes will be updated and provided through our blog at avicennacuisine.com. In the coming months, our team will also work to create a cookbook series based on trending topics, such as gluten free, non-GMO, and certified organic recipes to name a few.

I thought I should also mention to you that I come from a remarkable Iranian-American family. Since I began cooking at the age of 15, I have loved to entertain and host dinner parties for friends and family with the help of my mother, NPR Senior Producer, Davar Ardalan, always with a Persian twist. I've been raised on Persian food and have learned to cook almost all the traditional dishes, from juicy chicken kabob with rice and "bottom of the pan" yummy rice (tadigh) to slow cooked stews with barberries and saffron.

I also understand tastes and flavors and owe many of these skills to one of my mentors, Jerry Edwards. Jerry taught me so much during my time working for his catering company during my college internship at Chef's Expressions in Baltimore, MD. Jerry would host monthly wine dinners from his home where I had the opportunity to cook family style meals paired with delicious wines from around the world and from his travels. I also sat on the board of the Farm to Chef MD competition, a local culinary competition that benefits the Days of Taste where chefs and local farms would partner together to create innovative dishes for guests to enjoy. The food and hospitality industry fascinate me and although I am young, I have attended and worked hundreds of culinary experiences and read many books on food, health and nutrition to know what an individual in search of a diet or healthy lifestyle is looking for.

When I had the opportunity to work with my grandmother on writing this book, I did it first and foremost for her. To show her how much I love and appreciate her, but also to showcase an intriguing new culinary idea that could potentially change our lives and everyone around us.

According to the World Health Organization (WHO), Health is a state of complete physical, mental, and social well-being. Nowadays it is no surprise that health is no longer simply defined as just the absence of disease. Healthy Living is the actions, steps and plans one puts together to achieve optimum health. In addition, Healthy Living is about taking responsibility of our body and minds each and every day and making smart health choices for our future. This means eating right according to our particular Temperament, stay active and exercising regularly, sustaining emotional and spiritual wellness, and disease prevention are all a part of creating a healthy lifestyle. Since all aspects of one's self must work in harmony to attain wellness, we need to put balanced energy into all aspects of ourselves.

The body requires wholesome nutrition, proper weight, beneficial exercise, adequately balanced sleep, rest and wakefulness, and proper stress management. The mind needs positive attitudes, thoughts, perspectives and self-confidence. You also need to practice giving and receiving forgiveness,

compassion, and love; it is so important to laugh and live for joy and happiness with yourself and others. The Spiritual You requires inner peace, creativity, and trust within you. When our Physical Body is out of balance, our
body tells us right away. We feel fatigued, can catch a cold or even become
repeatedly ill.

Avicenna Cuisine will teach you how to understand your Temperament
to better understand what foods you should be eating that will help you to
develop a healthy lifestyle in combination with controlling your individual
Nurturing Essentials. I hope you love the book, and, if you have any questions or stories you would like to share on this topic, please e-mail us at
info@avicennacuisine.com.

ACKNOWLEDGEMENTS

IT IS WITH THE DEEPEST GRATITUDE that I acknowledge Kazi Publications in Chicago, Illinois for their extensive research and translation of the *Canon of Medicine*. My grandmother, Laleh Bakhtiar, Editor-at-large spent seven years on this project. Avicenna Cuisine would not have been made possible without her passion and dedication to showcase Avicennian Medicine to the world in English for the first time in 1,000 years.

I want to thank my beautiful and talented mother, Davar Ardalan who has always inspired me to be an independent, hardworking and innovative Iranian-American woman.

I am grateful each and everyday for my amazing friendship with my older brother, Saied. He is a mastermind who has always supported this project and given me invaluable guidance that every sister needs and desires.

To my lovely aunt, Mani Farhadi, whose creative and intelligent mind gave me the vital guidance and feedback I needed throughout this process.

To my uncle, Karim Ardalan, who illustrated his exceptional artistic talents in creating my website, www.avicennacuisine.com.

To my two stepfathers, John O. Smith and Faroukh Ardalan. Each in their own way encouraged me to believe in myself and follow my dreams.

To Aman and Amir, my two youngest brothers who I helped raise. Everyday I look forward to being there for them as they grow into courageous gentlemen.

To all my other family and close friends who I've had the pleasure of talking to and sharing my journey with. I sustain myself with the love from all of you and appreciate each of your advice and positive encouragement.

Last but not least, I'd like to thank God for all His visions and blessings.

INTRODUCTION

AVICENNA CUISINE IS A LOST ART, remnants of which are practiced throughout the East and the West, the North and South, without those who practice it knowing its source. The author, Samira Ardalan, has found the source in Avicenna's *Canon of Medicine*.[1]

I say "art" because, while the "science" of Avicenna is practiced in medical circles and educational institutions, the art of its use in cuisine has been lost until now. Avicenna Cuisine is based on a saying of Hippocrates: Food is your medicine and medicine is your food.

While current research places the origin of the humoural theory to have been that of the Zoroastrians (circa 1000 BCE),[2] it is believed that Hippocrates was to have furthered this theory that is the basis of Avicenna Cuisine. Avicenna Cuisine is based on four primary body fluid that may include or humours to be found in our blood, blood also being one of the humours. They are the blood humour (sanguine, hot and wet), yellow bile humour (choleric, bilious humour, hot and dry), phlegmatic humour (cold and wet) and black bile humour (melancholic, atrabilious humour, cold and dry).[3] The goal is to maintain a balanced system of humours that will result in good health.

The process whereby this goal is achieved is based on two principles: Eating the opposites and moderation or avoidance of extremes.

While traditional and alternative medicines exist to treat disease and illness, the connection to food and what we eat in many cultures has been forgotten. Without knowledge of the basis of the cuisine system for the development of a healthy lifestyle, its holistic nature disappears and what is left is an oral tradition perpetuated by grandmothers and aunts who say, for instance: "Don't eat fish with yogurt because they are both cold."[4]

According to Avicenna everything created is developed out of the atmospheric conditions of hot, cold, wet or dry just as our daily weather report tells us.[5]

The Elements

The elements from which the elemental qualities are derived are simple substances which are primary constituents of the human body. It is by their combination and appropriate organization that the various orders of things in nature have been formed.

Natural philosophy speaks of four primary elements. Two of these are light and two heavy. Fire and air are light while earth and water are heavy. Hot and cold are active qualities, according to Avicenna, and moist and dry are passive. He gives the reason for this: Dryness increases heat whereas moisture increases cold. Therefore, they are considered to be of secondary importance.[6]

The Humours

The elemental qualities reach a certain proportion of hot, cold, wet and dry to form within our blood what are called the four primary "humours" of yellow bile (hot and dry, also called choleric), black bile (cold and dry, also called atrabilious or melancholic), phlegmatic (cold and wet called phlegm) and blood (hot and wet, also called sanguine).

These humours form what we call temperament. Temperament is of two kinds: Inherent, the temperament with which we are born, our natural predisposition, and acquired, based on our nurturing process.

We may say that the "salt principle" of the body is the blood humour; the yellow bile humour the "bitter principle," the phlegmatic humour the "sweet principle," and the black bile humour "the sour principle" of the body.[7]

The primary fluids arise from out of the male and female sperm at the time of conception. Avicenna says that the qualities of hot, cold, wet and dry that form the humours come from our Innate Heat and radical moisture produced from: . . . two things: (1) the male semen and (2) the female "sperm."[8]

Innate Heat, Radical Moisture and Their Interaction[9]

Innate Heat has six functions: (1) It is a product of the Breath of Life; (2) it is first combusted in the heart along with the Breath of Life. There it takes on its form as Innate Heat. This Innate Heat is the basic body heat emitted by all the organs and tissues as a result of the metabolizing of the smallest living organisms or the cells; (3) it is carried with the Breath of Life by the blood to all organs and tissues in order to activate the metabolism of the cells; (4) Innate Heat in the liver is turned into metabolic heat which powers digestion in the natural power. Along with Breath of Life, Innate Heat generates the four humours. Innate Heat "cooks" the humours through a digestive process while the natural power empowers the functions of the humours; (5) Innate Heat in the brain is converted into nervous energy or heat that energizes a type of what can be called mental digestion through the processing of thoughts, ideas and experiences; (6) in the generative or reproductive energy, Innate Heat brings new life.

From middle age on, Innate Heat begins to decline. This is due to the dispersive effect of the atmospheric air on the moisture, which is the basic material for heat. The Innate Heat gradually disperses the body's moisture. The various secretions of the body are also constantly drying up from normal physical and emotional activity.

RADICAL MOISTURE

According to Avicenna, the material for growth, Radical Moisture cannot be altered or grown without an efficient cause, as explained by the author in the text. In this case, efficient cause is nature, which operates through the Innate Heat.

Avicenna describes four types of secondary body fluids, the primary being the humours. Secondary fluids of the body are either non-excrements or excrements. The non-excrements have not yet been subjected to any action by any of the simple organs and they are not changed until they reach the destined tissues. They are of four types: (1) that which is located at the orifices of the minutest channels near the tissues and thus irrigating them (Latin *cambium*, that is, vascular *cambium* forms tissues that carry water and nutrients throughout the body); (2) that which permeates the tissues like a dew and is capable of being transformed into nutriment if it becomes necessary (Latin *ros*); (3) the third type forms a nutrient which will be changed into the substance of the tissues, whether to the extent of entering into their temperament or to the extent of changing into their very essence, thereby attaining an entire likeness to the member or organ (Latin *gluten,* a grayish, sticky component); (4) the fourth type accounts for the continuous identity of the member or organ or of the body throughout one's life (Radical Moisture, Latin *humidum radicali*). It is derived from the semen, which in its turn is derived from the humours.

INTERACTION BETWEEN INNATE HEAT AND RADICAL MOISTURE

As we have seen according to Avicenna, the human being takes its origin from two things: (1) the male semen, which plays the part of form; and (2) the female "semen" (ovum), which provides the matter. Each of these is fluid and moist, but there is more wateriness and earthly substance in the female blood and female "sperm," whereas air and fire are predominant in the male sperm.

He remarks that is essential that at the outset of the congelation of the two components there should be Radical Moisture, even though earth and fire are found in the product. The earth provides the firmness and rigidity; the fire provides the power of maturation. These give the clot a certain hardness or firmness.

Our bodies are exposed to harm through the dispersion of Radical Moisture from which we have been created, This dispersion takes place gradually. The other type of harm comes from the breakdown that causes decay and transformation of the Radical Moisture into a form such that life is no longer able to proceed.

The second source of harm differs from the first in that dryness is here introduced by virtue of depravity of humour; and this dryness continues neutralizing the Radical Moisture of our body until our form ceases to have a capacity for life. Finally, the breakdown through decay disperses our vitality, because it first destroys the Radical Moisture and then disperses it, and simply dry ash is left behind.

Therefore, it is clear that these two sources of harm [of the living product of conception] are different from those arising from other causes—such as, freezing cold, torrid heat, grave forms of loss of continuity, various maladies.

Each of them take their origin from extrinsic and intrinsic agents. The extrinsic agents are, for example, the atmosphere, which is a solvent and decay-causing. The intrinsic agents are, for example, Innate Heat, which is the agent within us through which Radical Moisture is dispersed: the extraneous heat generated within us forms nutrients and food, and through other agents which cause decaying changes in our [natural] Radical Moisture.

All these agents mutually aid one another in rendering our body dry. While it is true that our perfection and soundness and the power to perform our various actions depend on a degree of dryness of our blood, but the degree of dryness becomes relatively greater and greater until we die. Therefore, this dryness is inevitable.

If we were at the outset essentially composed of Radical Moisture, heat would have to overcome it or else the heat would be choked by it. Therefore, the heat continues to exert its own effect, that is, it produces more and more dryness. But whatever degree of dryness there might be at the outset of life, it reaches equilibrium, and remains so until the limit of equilibrium in regard to dryness is reached. The heat remaining constant, the dryness is now relatively greater than before for the matter is less, and hence holds more.

Therefore, it is not difficult to understand that the dryness passes on beyond the stage of equilibrium and goes on steadily increasing until the whole of the Radical Moisture of the body is consumed. Therefore, Avicenna says that the Innate Heat is the cause of its own extinction, for it is itself the reason for its own matter being consumed.

Radical Moisture, then, must come to an end and Innate Heat is extinguished. This occurs sooner if another contributory factor to destruction is present similar to the extraneous excess of humour arising out of the imperfect digestion of food. This extinguishes the Innate Heat by smothering it, enclosing it and by providing the contrary quality. This extraneous humour is called the cold, phlegmatic humour. That is how natural or physiological death ensues. The duration of life depends on the original temperament, that retains a certain degree of power to the end by fostering its Radical Moisture. (Death from accident or illness has, however, a different origin. Whether from physiological or pathological cause, it is, of course, ultimately determined in accordance with one's fate or destiny).

The dryness (of the body) is increased in two ways: by lessening of the ability to receive matter or by the lessening of the Radical Moisture resulting from dispersal of the Innate Heat. The heat becomes more feeble because dryness predominates in the substance of the members, and because the Radical Moisture becomes relatively less.

Avicenna compares the Radical Moisture to the Innate Heat as the oil of a lamp is to the flame. For there are two forms of Radical Moisture in the flame: water, which holds its own, and oil, which is used up. So, in a corresponding manner, the Innate Heat holds its own in respect of the Radical Moisture, but is used up on equal footing with the increase of extraneous heat, due, for example, to defective digestion, which is comparable with the Radical Moisture of the flame. As the dryness increases, the Innate Heat lessens, and the result is natural death.

The reason why the human body does not live any longer than it does lies in the fact that the initial Radical Moisture holds out against being dispersed both by the alien heat and by the heat in the body itself (both that which is Innate and that derived from bodily movement). And this resistance is maintained as long as the one is weaker than the other and as long as something is provided to replace that which has been thus dispersed, to wit, from the nutriment or food. Furthermore, as we have already stated, the power or drive that operates upon the food and sustenance in order to render it useful in this way only does so up to the end of life.

Therefore, Avicenna says that the art of maintaining health is not the art of averting death or of averting extraneous injuries from the body or of securing the utmost longevity possible to the human being. It is concerned with two other things: (1) the prevention of breakdown from decay; and (2) the safeguarding of Radical Moisture from too rapid dissipation and maintaining it at such a degree of strength that the original type of temperament peculiar to the person shall not change even up to the last moment of life.

He asserts that this is secured by a suitable diet, namely: (a) one which will ensure the replacement, as exactly as possible, of the Innate Heat and Radical Moisture which are dispersed from the body as exactly as possible; and (b) a diet which will prevent any agents which would lead to a rapid drying from gaining the upper hand excluding agents which produce a normal dryness; (c) one which safeguards the body from the development of decay-causing processes within it and from the influence of alien heat (whether extraneous or intrinsic) because all bodies do not have the same degree of Radical Moisture and Innate Heat. There is a great diversity in regard to them. Moreover, every person has his own term of life, during which the drying up process is inevitable to his temperament.

There are two drives to be fostered in striving for this object as indicated by Avicenna: (1) the nutritive drive whereby what is constantly being lost to the body is replaced, namely cold and dry (earthiness) and Radical Moisture; and (2) the sensitive Vital Energy that is concerned with the replacement of that which is lost to the body, namely air (hot and wet) and fire (hot and dry). And since food and sustenance are only potentially like the thing nourished, the digestive assistants had to be created so that they could be changed actually into the likeness of the thing nourished. In this way the food becomes effective.

The instruments and channels necessary for this had to be created also—namely the means by which material is attracted, digested, retained, and expelled sequence by sequence, turn by turn.

Therefore, he says that the essential considerations in the art of preserving the health consist in maintaining balance and equilibrium between all these various occurring factors. But there are seven matters concerning which special care must be expended to ensure just proportion: (1) balance of temperament; (2) selection of the articles of food and drink; (3) evacuation of effete matters; (4) safeguarding the chyme; (5) maintaining the purity of the air respired; (6) guarding against extraneous contingencies; and (7) moderation in regard to the movements of the body and the motions of the mind, which includes sleep and wakefulness.

From all these considerations, Avicenna states that one will now perceive that there is no single fixed limit to which balance or health is to be assigned. Health and balance vary (in range) from time to time. That is to say, it is a state comprised within two limits.

> It may be summarized that both children and the young are balanced in regard to heat, while the middle aged and the senile are relatively cold-tempered. Children, however, possess a moderate excess of moisture to fulfill the requirements of growth. The excess of moisture in children is evident from the softness of their bones and nerve tissues and also from the fact that it has not been long since they grew and developed from the semen, blood and ethereal Vital Energy. The middle-aged and the old are not only cold, but also dry. This can be observed from their bones being hard and the skin dry, and inferred from the long time having elapsed since they originally developed from the blood, semen and ethereal Vital Energy. Both the children and the young adults are fiery to the same extent. There is more water and air in children than in the youth. The middle-aged and, particularly, the old and senile show a larger amount of cold and dryness in their constitution than children and the young adults, but the young are more balanced than children. The grownups are, however, drier than children and hotter than the old and the middle-aged. On the other hand, elderly persons are drier than the young and middle-aged persons in their primary temperamental constitution. They are, however, more moist because of the abnormal moisture which makes their tissues temporarily and superficially moist.[10]

TEMPERAMENT

There are many words used to describe our temperament such as personality, constitution and so forth. Whatever term is used, it is a well-known truth that each one of us is on a journey to "know our 'self'", to know the what, where, who, when and why we think, feel and act the way that we do and to recognize the universal truth that the only person we can change is our "self."

To summarize Avicenna Cuisine, we could outline it in the following way, the details of which will follow through the chapters of this work by the author as we try to understand what answers Avicenna was seeking.[11]

In regard to the Avicenna and answers he was searching for, he was most interested in investigating the causes of changes in living bodies and the activities in which they engage. He reasoned that living bodies that can move because of their own will must have causes that distinguish them from things that do not move from their own volition.

He searched for the cause:

[This art] is primarily interested in the cause (or causes) belonging to living bodies that explains that set of activities unique to them as living. Thus, Avicenna begins by pointing out that it is simply a matter of empirical observation that certain bodies sensibly perceive and move about voluntarily, as well as they are able to take in nourishment, grow and reproduce.

These activities cannot belong to them simply in as much as they are bodies, for otherwise all bodies would manifest these activities, which they clearly do not. A stone may be split in two or fall to the ground, but no one would say that in such cases it has reproduced or moved around of its own will. Given this difference between the natural activities of different kinds of bodies, living bodies must have some other principle or cause in addition to their mere corporeality.[12]

This principle he calls the "soul" [or mind]. For Avicenna, the word "soul" is simply:

. . . .a word to indicate that thing or things, whatever it or they might be, that living bodies have that non-living bodies lack and on account of which living bodies do those activities that define them as living.[13]

The soul is known by observing change:

. . . .we may not know what the soul is, but we know it exists, because we can see what it does. [Our health] can also reveal other truths about the soul, such as the location of its various parts in the brain, heart and liver, or its transmission through the nerves. Different aspects of the soul exhibit different 'powers', i.e., causal postulates conceived in relation to their specific effects. Thus, the soul can be a proper object of scientific inquiry if one concentrates on its evident manifestation and seeks to make causal and categorical sense of them within a general theory of functioning.[14]

NATURAL SCIENCE

Avicenna's Natural Science included the study of the bodies of which the universe is composed: the heavens and the stars in the macrocosm and the simple elements of earth, air, fire and water and their elemental properties of hot, cold, moist and dry as well as the compound bodies of minerals, plants, animals and human beings; how they change, develop and intermix.

Natural [Science] is that aspect of wisdom that deals with the domain that moves and changes. It is the study, at once quantitative and qualitative, of that which is an accident and constitutes, along with mathematics and metaphysics, the domain of [theoretical] philosophy. The branches of natural philosophy constitute all the sciences of the sublunary region [the world of generation and corruption] including that of the sciences of medicine, [cuisine and ethics].[15]

For Avicenna, the human being is a microcosm of the macrocosmic universe. As with other traditional scientists, he follows two cardinal doctrines:

. . . .namely the hierarchic structure of the cosmos and the correspondence between the microcosm and the macrocosm.[16]

In his view, the human body is the instrument used by our soul [mind] and the spirit [energy] that make up the human being's inner world connecting them outwardly through the grades of the hierarchy of the macrocosm back to the Source of cosmic manifestation. "Likewise, he sought the principles of medicine [and cuisine] in the sciences dealing with the Principle and its manifestations."[17]

THE WORLD OF GENERATION AND CORRUPTION

The unfolding of the human soul in the world of generation and corruption begins with the role of the four elements and their elemental properties in creating 'matter".

[The world of generation and corruption is] a world in which the soul and matter are united empowering living objects at various levels. In contrast to the heavens where separate things like the ideas or thoughts or angels can exist without matter, the condition of existence in the sublunary world requires the existence of matter for every form and the existence of form for all matter. In fact, it is this necessity that causes continuous change.[18]

According to Avicenna, each body acquires a particular soul and every soul in-forms a particular body. This, then, gives the soul its particular individuality, as every living object is "in-formed" matter. Human nature is in-formed matter, bearing certain properties or marks and endowed with existence. Each organ in the body is in-formed matter. Every tissue is in-formed matter. The blood, the lymph, the urine, etc, are each in-formed matter. Every microscopic cell of which the tissues are composed is merely in-formed matter. So also is every chemical entity that composes the cells, and the whole person also is just in-formed matter.

As a result of the movement of the forces of nature in the sub-lunar region, Avicenna explains that a great deal of heat was generated:

. . . .and from the heat the separation of the [elements] of this region was brought about. The separation in turn caused dryness; hence a substance called fire, possessing the qualities of heat and dryness, came into being. Whatever remained of the [remaining elements] fell away from the heavens toward the center. Unable to move, it became cold; the cold quality caused opaqueness and subsequently dryness.

Out of these qualities of dryness and cold, the element earth was formed. Whatever of the [elements] remained was bound by the earth below and fire above. The half near the fire became warm without there being any separation among its parts since the heat was not excessive. Therefore, a new element comprised of the qualities of heat and moisture called air, came into being. The other half near the earth became cold, but since this coldness was not excessive, it did not condense, so that an element consisting of the qualities of moisture and cold, called water, was formed. In this way the four principles of all sublunary bodies were generated.

The progressive 'coagulation' of the [elements] terminates with extreme differentiation, and the process of emanation reaches its terminal point. Henceforth the movement is no longer a drawing away from the principle, but a return to it, not an emanation, but a love, by which all things are attracted to the source of all Being.

The elements in mixing together reach a degree of harmony that permits the descent of the lowest form of soul upon them. This descent brings into being the minerals enlivened by the mineral soul and the power to preserve forms. This is the lowest kingdom of the physical domain. In the mineral kingdom itself, subtleness increases until in the jewels, the highest members of this domain, the 'fire of the soul' is much stronger than in stones or mud.

In the coral, the first stage of the plant kingdom is reached [enlivened by the plant or vegetative soul [Natural Energy] and the powers of self-nourishment, growth and reproduction]. The increase in [perfection] of the mixture of elements permits a new soul, or more precisely a new [power] of the soul to descend upon it. This new [power], and not the elements or their manner of combination, is responsible for the characteristics that distinguish the plant world from the mineral. In the plant kingdom, also, there is a hierarchy in which [perfection] increases, reaching its highest degree in the palm tree, which already possesses certain features of animals.

With increasing [perfection] in the mixing of the elements, again a new [power] of the soul—this time called the animal soul [Neural Energy] [and the powers of motivation and sensation/perception]—enters the stage of the cosmic play and manifests itself in ever greater degree from the snail to the monkey, which even resembles the human being in certain of his features.

The hierarchy of being rises with the degree of [perfection] to the stages of the human being. . . . In each case a new soul or [the power] of the soul comes into play [where the soul evolves into spirit or intellect]. There are also stages above that of humanity, including the stage of the spiritual soul through which the Active Intellect is reached, and finally the highest stage, that of the saints and prophets, which itself comprises numerous angelic worlds.[19]

It is here in the sublunary world that the Giver of Forms, a separate intelligence and an immaterial substance, gives substantial forms to properly prepared primary matter formed in the father and mother's semen. The properly prepared primary matter of living bodies (other than the human being) consists of the elements and their elemental qualities. The properly prepared primary matter that will take on a human form consists of undifferentiated humours (the humours playing the basic role within the human form similar to the role of the elements in the sublunary world).

When the human male sperm and female ova unite in creating an embryo, the embryo receives the substantial form of the human soul from the Giver of Forms. The Giver of Forms activates the Breath of Life, Innate Heat and Radical Moisture from the undifferentiated humour. Avicenna says:[20]

The Breath of Life enables the powers of the soul to be conveyed into the corresponding organs and members. In the first place the Breath of Life is the rallying point for the powers of the soul, and in the second place it is an emanation into the various members and tissues of the body.[21]

The Giver of Forms produced the Breath of Life out of the finer particles of the humours and out of fieriness (heat and dryness); and, at the same time, produced the tissues themselves out of the coarser and earthy (cold and dry) particles of these humours. In other words, the Breath of Life is related to the thinner particles as the body is related to the coarser particles of the same humours.

The beginning of the Breath of Life is as an emanation from potentiality to actuality proceeding without intermission or stint until the form is completed and perfected.

The Breath of Life enters the heart where it undergoes combustion and circulates throughout the embryo through its blood stream.

The Breath of Life produces three energies (spirits): Vital, Natural and Neural. The Vital Energy enters the heart; the Natural Energy enters the liver; and the Neural Energy enters the brain. These three energies cause the humours to separate into the four humours. Each of the humours has a pair of the elemental qualities (blood: hot and wet; yellow bile: hot and dry; phlegm: cold and wet; black bile: cold and dry) that form the temperament of the body. These three energies activate the powers or drives of the human soul.

The human soul includes the power of the mineral soul to preserve shape or form; the powers of the plant soul of growth, reproduction and nutrition and nutrition's four secondary powers of attraction, digestion, retention and evacuation; and the powers of the animal/human soul.

The powers of the animal/human soul include the power of motion/motivation and the power of sensation/perception. Within the human soul, the power of motivation along with the power of motion includes the concupiscent and the irascible powers, the latter two known as "the passions." The animal/human soul's power of sensation includes the five external powers of seeing, hearing, smelling, tasting and touching. The powers of perception include the five internal powers: common sense, retention, estimation, memory and imagination. Imagination divides into two powers: sensation (all animals) and rational (human being only).

When speaking about the powers that use the body as its instrument to effect change, motion or motivation, the word "soul" is used. When the soul's powers are involved with intellection and estimation, they are called "intellects" as the soul is potentially "intellect." When the intellect receives intuitive illumination, it is called the "spiritual" heart, intellect or soul.

The rational intellect is divided into two parts: the theoretical intellect and the practical intellect. The theoretical intellect has four levels— material, habitual, actual and acquired intellects. The acquired intellect can ascend to the level of the spiritual soul/intellect that is that of the prophets and saints. The theoretical intellect, directed upwards to receive ideas, is activated by the Active Intellect (the Active Intellect is to ideas what the

Giver of Forms is to forms). The practical intellect, directed downwards and under the direction of the theoretical intellect, governs the body.

As only the human soul is rational and contains all of the powers of the soul, it is considered to be potentially the soul in its most complete and perfect form. This is why Rumi can speak of the various grades of the soul moving towards completion and perfection. In other words, it is the soul within living beings that evolves through change as Rumi indicates:

> I died from mineral and plant became;
> Died from the plant and took a sentient frame;
> Died from the beast and donned a human dress;
> When by my dying did I e'er grow less:
> Another time from manhood I must die
> To soar with angel-pinions through the sky.
> 'Midst angels also I must lose my place.
> Since 'Everything shall perish save His Face.'
> Let me be Naught! The harp-strings tell me plain
> That unto Him do we return again! [22]

The major roles of the rational intellect, also known as reason, are to control the irrational animal powers known as the passions: concupiscence (attraction to pleasure, lust) and irascibility (avoidance of harm/pain, anger). The struggle of reason with the passions is considered by Avicenna to be the Final Cause of the soul.

Based on this view, the author describes Avicenna's seven nature-given essentials and the six nurture-given necessities.

For Avicenna Cuisine, the next important understanding is that of dietetics, the systematic control of food and drink to conserve health or combat disease,[23] and digestion for which he gives a complete picture of the importance of this vital process to human life. Instead of emphasis upon the brain or the heart, it is the liver that is the center of cuisine as this is what supplies us with our energy and in this system of cuisine, the chef is as a physician.

> What . . . is the difference in intention between the man who discovered the mode of life suitable for the sick, who is called a physician and admitted to be a scientist, and him who, from the beginning, discovered the way to prepare the food we now eat instead of the former wild and animal-like diet? I can see no difference; the discovery is one and the same thing.[24]

Although he then insists that the physician is the forerunner of the chef, what he accurately identified was a medico-culinary tradition, or rather, a tradition in which medical and culinary concerns for food and nourishment were assumed to be closely joined. It is in this broader sense that dietetics should properly be viewed.[25]

Foods that we eat and drinks we consume [each also has a temperament as the author shows in her last chapter] must be prepared in such a way that they are healthy and beneficial to our specific temperament. Ingredients have to be adjusted so that it complements or even counterbalances our individual temperaments so that a balance can be either maintained or, alternatively, attained in the case of an imbalanced temperament.

> For instance, [lamb is] manipulated as follows: it is cooked with vinegar . . . when rarefying and cooling effects [are] sought. However, it [is] cooked with a . . . liquid fermented sauce [similar to soy sauce] when rarefying effects and speedy digestion [are] needed. When the aim [is] only to cool down the dish's properties, it [is] cooked with yogurt, whey, sumac, or pomegranate . . . . A chef is expected to delight . . . with recipes of delicious foods and tell them how to maintain or restore their health through proper diet . . . . He touches on the four human humours, and the recommended foods for each type. He discusses the humoural properties and powers of foods. He understands regulating the meals according to the seasons of the year, the recommended dishes for different ailments, the benefits of exercise before the meal, and avoiding the harms of food. After all these informative and cautionary chapters, cooking begins. Digestives and medicinal comforting drinks, pastes, conserves, and condensed juices are also dealt with. He deals with the benefits of sleep on the digestive system.
>
> This theory is applied in cooking to produce the best results. For instance, iron pans, which are cold in nature, are recommended for frying fish, which has cold properties. The cold properties of pan and fish will be counterbalanced by the hot properties of fire and the frying oil.
>
> Each entity in nature is composed of a specific combination of these qualities, which in a normal and healthy state is deemed proper and unique to it. Compared with other entities in nature, human beings are, relatively speaking, the most temperate (balanced).[26]

In terms of achieving a balance, Avicenna points out in this text:

> However, balance in the human body does not mean that these properties are equally divided in quantity. Rather, it means that the body has its proper proportions, which may be within a wide range that spans perfect balance

(50/50), plausible only theoretically, and the points where the human temperance/balance starts to lean towards excess or deficiency. The state of having excess or deficiency in properties is described as having an imbalanced temperament that is no longer healthy and needs to be adjusted to its normal state. This can be partly achieved by having the right kinds of food. For instance, people with excessively cold temperaments can make up for deficiency in heat by having foods with hot properties like sweet dishes. Similarly, foods with cold properties can be manipulated by adding to them a hot spice like black pepper to make them more balanced.[27]

According to Avicenna, it is our Innate Heat that digests our food from which our humours are produced. This process of digestion is like cooking, our stomach being our stove. If we have a moderate amount of heat, our humours will be able to nourish our body. If our digestive system produces too much heat, our liver will generate bad yellow bile (bilious or choleric) humour. If our liver produces an excessive amount of heat because we ate the wrong foods, the result is bad black bile (atrabilious or melancholic) humour. If our liver does not produce enough heat, the result is phlegm or phlegmatic humour or atrabilious (black bile) due to the fact that freezing and the solidification of liquids result from excessive cold. Avicenna further explains this in the present text.

In regard to digestion:

Cooking produces froth, analogous to the froth of blood, called 'yellow bile,' which is light and thin. This is normal and harmless. However, when heat is excessive, it causes burning, which is neither healthy nor good. Like burnt food, the humours' chyme will be spoiled. Abnormal harmful yellow bile is caused by too much heat, especially in the liver. The resulting burnt thin froth is bad yellow bile caused by over-indulging in foods that are hot in properties, low in density, sweet, fatty, or pungent.

Cooking also produces sediments, analogous to the sediments of blood, called 'black bile,' which is heavy and dense. This is normal and harmless. However, as in the case of yellow bile, when heat is excessive, it causes burning, which is neither healthy nor good, because the humours' chyme will be spoiled. The burnt sediments are bad black bile. Foods that are very dense and dry contribute to it, and if they are hot in properties, they will even be more so, resulting in sediments that do not flow or disintegrate and cause blockages. Black bile is caused by too hot a liver, too weak a spleen, excessive coldness, prolonged congestions or blockages, or prolonged sickness that causes the humours to burn. If too much black bile is generated between the stomach and the liver, there will be deficiency in blood and humours.

The undercooked humour, 'phlegm,' is unripe blood. Potentially it can turn into good blood if it is given enough heat, and does not stay for long in this state. Furthermore, eating foods that are dense, moist, thick, and cold cause 'phlegm.' 28

As Ardalan shows in III: Six-Nurturing Essentials, Avicenna Cuisine is based on a variety of foods each one of which suits our particular temperament. She states, "Food and drink are the easiest of the six nurture-given essentials for us to control. Clearly, a lack of moderation by eating too much food or drinking too many liquids that are the same as our dominant temperament will have a negative impact on us."

She then goes on to show the affects of the weather and how it aids in digestion, the best time for exercise or physical activity, the drinking of liquids, rest and sleep after eating, the order in which food should be eaten and both the quality and quantity of food on our digestive system. She then concludes that based on the Six Nurturing Essentials, we need to first know the temperament of our own body and then the temperament of the foods that we eat in order to help our digestion "cook" this food and avoid any harm that the wrong tempered food may cause us.

Temperament of the Foods and Drinks that We Consume

Therefore, to be able to adjust the properties of food to avoid any harm it might incur upon us as we consume it, we need to familiarize our "self" with the temperaments and powers of foodstuffs and drinks, as well as our particular temperament.

Ardalan then gives an in-depth understanding of the various temperaments. There are four primary and four balanced, compound temperaments and eight imbalanced where we may have both a primary and a secondary temperament that combines heat, cold, wetness or dryness creating a balance. Taking the Avicenna Cuisine Temperament Test will indicate which type we are followed by explanation of what each type, primary or secondary is, the strengths of each type and the weaknesses.

The last chapter of Avicenna Cuisine is perhaps the most important for us to understand as this is what has been lost to the West's understanding and, therefore, the practice of Avicenna Cuisine. This is, not only do each and every one of us have a particular temperament with some elements shared with others, but everything that we eat also has a temperament. It is just as important to understand the temperament of what we consume as it is to understand our own temperament.

It is the hope that with this Guidebook to Avicenna Cuisine, we will be able to live healthier and longer lives.

ENDNOTES TO THE INTRODUCTION

1 Avicenna (Abu Ali al-Husayn ibn Abd Allah ibn Sina, also known as Bu Ali) (973-1037 CE) had had access to Arabic translations of the earliest medical textbooks including those of Hippocrates (460-ca 370BCE) and Galen (ca 100 CE). He built upon their knowledge and that of Aristotle and then added his own invaluable experiences and wrote his monumental *Canon of Medicine* (the complete English translation of the five volumes has been published in 2015 by Kazi Publications). The Latin translation in the 13th century CE of the *Canon* became the most important medical textbook for training European physicians and chefs for 600 years. However, the origin of this idea has been lost because the *Canon of Medicine* of Avicenna that was alive and vibrant for over 600 years in Europe was not translated until today into modern languages nor was it made accessible in its original Arabic and studied except for a few pockets of what is called *Unani* (Greek) medicine in South East Asia. However, even there, the practitioners of this system of health do not have access to the complete *Canon* in their own language.

2 See http://zoroastrianheritage.blogspot.com/2011/07/irani-zarathushti-traditions-health.html

3 Yes, Hippocrates played an important part in the development of the humoural theory, but unfortunately most of his works have been lost. The next great exponent of the system was Galen (129-200/216 CE). While Galen did much to develop the Hippocratic system, he was not able to write in a way that brought about understanding of it. We would have to ask: why was the work of Galen not chosen as a medical textbook in Europe for 600 years? Instead, the medieval Europeans chose Avicenna and his work that was translated into Latin in the 13th century. Can we say it was because of Avicenna's genius to be able to explain the entire Hippocratic-Galenic humoural system in a way that was practical and useful to the development of the science of medicine? In the *Canon* Avicenna often refers to Hippocrates and Galen so he is open about his sources, but he was the first to experiment extensively with the various herbs and plants that he prescribed as medications or foods.

It should be noted that Fåhræus (1921), a Swedish physician who devised the erythrocyte sedimentation rate, suggested that the four humours were based upon the observation of blood clotting in a transparent container. When blood is drawn in a glass container and left undisturbed for about an hour, four different layers can be seen. A dark clot forms at the bottom (the "black bile"). Above the clot is a layer of red blood cells (the "blood"). Above this is a whitish layer of white blood cells (the "phlegm", now called the buffy coat). The top layer is clear yellow serum (the "yellow bile").

4 According to the Zoroastrians: Balance in Food Type—Hot and Cold [Tempered Foods]: "[There is] an age-old tradition [that] there are two types of food [temperaments]—hot/heating (*garmi*) or cold/cooling (*sardi*). There are those foods that are generally balanced between the two, and then there are restorative hot and cold-[tempered] foods designed to address an imbalance and thereby restore balance in the body. The concept is similar to yin and yang in Chinese food classification. The person making this determination is of necessity an experienced and knowledgeable healer, often an older woman in the community.

"Perhaps hot and cold-[temperaments] refer to the manner the body utilizes these foods, and whether they perk up or slow down a person physically, mentally and spiritually. Some say that hot [-tempered] foods thicken the blood while cold[-tempered] foods thin the blood. In what might sound like an anomaly in English, hot[-tempered] foods may produce cold sores in those so prone.

"An excess of cold[-tempered] foods is considered particularly dangerous for a person's health and can be found at the root of many 'circulation' related problems. Therefore, fish eaten with yogurt is a combination of two 'cold'[-tempered] foods that can cause problems. Worse is a super cold[-tempered] combination of yogurt and watermelon. Anecdotally, eating a lot of yogurt followed by watermelon is a cold cocktail potent enough to bring on a heart attack.

"While this may seem a contradiction, another tradition is to avoid an excess of 'cold'[-tempered] foods in hot weather and 'hot'[-tempered] foods in cold weather. The contradiction is the popular Iranian yogurt-cucumber drink taken to cool down in hot weather. Overdoing the consumption of such a beverage in hot weather may cause problems. Perhaps, it is an issue of degree.

The balance of hot and cold[-tempered] foods in their preparation makes for balance in aesthetics, taste and properties—and all of these properties are essential elements of good Iranian-Zoroastrian cuisine. For instance, in the preparation of *fesenjun*, a sauce for chicken dishes made from pomegranate juice and walnuts, walnuts are hot[-tempered] food, and pomegranate juice is a cold[-tempered] food. They are combined in order to provide balance. A meal of 'hot'[-tempered] kebabs is likewise balanced with 'cold' yoghurt and cucumber, cheese and vegetable relish such as [-tempered] radishes and parsley. 'Cold'[-tempered] pickles serve a similar purpose in helping to neutralize the effects of 'hot' fatty foods. See http://zoroastrianheritage.blogspot.com/2011/07/irani-zarathushti-traditions-health.html

Afghans also believe food is elemental in nature, and can produce hot or cold, or be neutral in the body.

http://www.afghan-web.com/culture/cooking/

"For Iranians: Although most meals will offer bread, rice, and meat (often a kebab), they often choose what foods will be served by following a set of food rules that originated from ancient practices. Foods are classified as either 'hot'[-tempered] or 'cold,'[-tempered] depending on the food's heating or cooling effect on the individual (rather than the food's actual temperature). Hot[-tempered] foods include meats, sweets, and eggplant. Yogurt, cucumbers, and fish classify as cold[-tempered]. Iranians try to serve a balance of hot and cold[-tempered] foods."
See http://www.foodbycountry.com/

Then there are interesting studies done about the dietary restrictions of pregnant women in Indonesia. In Madura in Indonesia "hot" food and drinks are forbidden during the first months of pregnancy. As soon as the movements of the fetus are felt "cool" food and drinks are preferred to those classified as "hot".

"In India (Andhra Pradesh) some pregnant women refuse to eat eggs and meat because they believe that these are "hot" foods. In Bangladesh especially, there are restrictions of "sour" or "hot" foods, but also of fat foods, meat, honey, certain fish, pulses and other foods. In Latin America, foods are similarly categorized in terms of "hot" and "cold". For example in the central region of Mexico, pregnant women are not allowed to eat tripe, chocolate or chili peppers towards the end of pregnancy because these foods are considered to be too "hot" and irritant. In Guatemala [people: Mayan Indians] indigenous midwives may prohibit pregnant women eating especially "cold" foods.

"Similar taboos also exist on foods during the antenatal period in Africa, Asia and Latin America." See *Indigenous Customs in Childbirth and Child Care* by Yvonne Lefèber, H. W. A. Voorhoeve. Publisher Van Gorcum https://webwinkel.vangorcum.nl/NL_toonBoek.asp?PublID=224) 1998

5 Avicenna, *Canon of Medicine*, Volume 1: *General Medicine*. Chicago: Kazi Publications, 1999, §25-31.

6 Avicenna, *Canon of Medicine*, Volume 1, §1807.

7 Gruner notes, *Canon of Medicine*, Volume 1.

8 According to Avicenna, death occurs when the body uses up all its Radical Moisture. See Avicenna, *Canon of Medicine*, Volume 1, §65-68)

9 Laleh Bakhtiar, *Avicenna's Psychology: A Textbook on Perennial Psychology*, Chicago: Institute of Traditional Psychology, 2013, p 4 ff.

10 Avicenna, *Canon of Medicine*, Volume 1.

11 Amber Haque (2004). "Psychology from an Islamic Perspective: Contributions of Early Muslim Scholars and Challenges to Contemporary Muslim Psychologists." Journal of Religion and Health 43 (4): 357-377 [3760 (AH).

12 Avicenna, *Kitab al-Shifa*, I.1.

13 Avicenna. (2010). *Kitab al-najat*, "Psychology," 1, 318.2-4, Jon McGinnis, (JM), p. 92.

14 R.J. Hankinson. (2009). "Medicine and the Science of the Soul," Can Bull Med Hist. 26(1):129-154.

14: Hart GD (December 2001). "Descriptions of blood and blood disorders before the advent of laboratory studies." Br. J. Haematol. 115 (4): 719–28. doi:10.1046/j.1365-2141.2001.03130.x. PMID 11843802.

15 Seyyed Hossein Nasr. (1993). *Introduction to Islamic Cosmological Doctrines*, p 215.

16 Seyyed Hossein Nasr. (1976). *Introduction to Islamic Science: An Illustrated Study*, Chicago: Kazi Publications, 1999, p. 160.

17 *Ibid.*, p. 159.

18 Avicenna. (1331/1952). *Danishnamah-yi Ala al-Dawlah* (Book of Science Dedicated to Ala al-Dawlah), Ilahiyat, pp. 134-135. Seyyed Hossein Nasr, p. 240.

19 Avicenna. (1331/1952). *Risalah Dar Haqiqat wa Kaifiyat-i Silsila-yi Mawjudat wa Tasalsul-i Asbab wa Musabbabat*, pp. 24-25. Seyyed Hossein Nasr, pp. 206-207.

20 Avicenna, *Canon of Medicine*, Volume 1, "On the Breath."

21 The following text is from Laleh Bakhtiar, *Avicenna's Psychology: A Textbook on Perennial Psychology*, Chicago: Institute of Traditional Psychology, 2013, p 4 ff.

22 Jalal al-Din Rumi. (1906). *Masnavi*, 3:218. Translated by E. G. Browne, *A Literary History of Persia*.

23 See W F Bynum, E J Browne, and Roy Porter (eds), *Dictionary of the History of Science*, London, Macmillan, 1981, p 102)

24 *Hippocratic Writings*, ed. with an introduction by G E R Lloyd, Harmondsworth, Penguin [1950], 1983, p 72 (translation of Tradition in medicine, pp. 70-86, by J Chadwick and W M Mann.

25 David Waines, "Dietetics in Medieval Islamic Culture," *Medical History*, 1999, 43: 228-240

26 *Annals of the Caliphs' Kitchen*, translated by Nawal Nasrallah, Introduction, Leiden, Netherlands: E. J. Brill, 2010.

27 *Ibid.*

28 *Ibid.*

PART I

The Seven Nature-Given Essentials

Avicenna Cuisine recognizes the following seven nature-given essentials in approaching a healthy, balanced lifestyle.

CHAPTER 1

The Elements

WHAT ARE THE FOUR ELEMENTS?

ACCORDING TO AVICENNA CUISINE, every living being is composed of "the four elements" of earth, air, fire and water. These "elements" are not "material," but rather have a virtual existence resulting in the various states of matter and how they function, namely, solids, liquids, gases and plasma.

Therefore, a difference should be observed between them and the literal meaning of: earth, water, air and fire and what we mean here.

Fire that burns is not the element of fire, but in another shape. Whatever is fixed is of the element of earth. Whatever nourishes is from the element of air and whatever consumes is from the element of water. Growth belongs to the element of fire. Where that element fails, there is no increment. Except the element of earth supplied it, there would be no end to growth. This fixes it. That is to say, it supplies an end for the element of fire. So, also, unless the elements of air are present, no nutrition could be brought about (i.e. oxygen). All things are nourished by air alone. Again, nothing can be dissolved or consumed unless the element of water be the cause. By it all things are mortified and reduced to nothing.[1]

Each one of the "elements" contains something of the other, the correspondingly named element being merely preponderant. Each of these elements possesses its own inherent or innate quality or "natural pre-disposition" with which it was created. It is by the combination and appropriate organization of the four "elements" that the various orders of things in nature have been formed.

AIR

Air is a simple substance that lies above water and beneath fire. This is due to its relative lightness. Its effect and value in the world of creation is to rarefy and render things finer, lighter, more delicate, softer, and consequently better able to move to the higher spheres.

FIRE

Fire is a simple substance whose natural position is above all the other elements. Thus, in nature it is located in that region of the sublunary world, hence, its absolute lightness. It matures, rarefies, refines, and intermingles with all things. Its penetrative power enables it to traverse the substance of the air. With this power it subsumes the coldness of the two heavy cold elements. By this power it rings the elementary properties into harmony.

EARTH

Earth is a simple substance whose normal location is in the center of existence. In this position it remains stationary, but when away from the center, it tends to return to its normal position. This is the reason for its intrinsic weight. These qualities of the earth can be easily appreciated by our senses as long as there is no interference by extraneous agents and it obeys its particular nature. It is by means of the element of earth that the parts of our body are fixed and held together into a compacted form. This is how our outward form is maintained.

Water

Water is a simple substance that in its natural state surrounds the earth and is, in its turn, surrounded by the air, subject, of course, to the other elements being also present in their own natural positions. This positioning is because of its relative density. It appears to our senses as long as there are no influences to counteract it. It lends itself readily to dispersion and therefore assumes any shape without permanency. It allows things to be molded and spread out and moderate in their construction because, quite unlike the earth, it easily parts with its old shape and readily accepts a new one.

Elemental Qualities

For Avicenna Cuisine, it is the natural qualities of the elements that are vital to a healthy lifestyle. These natural qualities are constantly in a state of change. It is the change that is the important thing, not the elements themselves, for matter, after all, only exists by virtue of the ceaselessly acting creative power of nature. We are apt to be deceived by "matter" and devote our thoughts to this instead of to the changes.

To be balanced and centered means that we are balanced in terms of the natural qualities of the elements which are hot, cold, wet and dry—which combine together to make four more possibilities: hot and dry, hot and wet, cold and dry, cold and wet.

The Qualities

The Qualities of Air are Hot and Wet

The nature of air is hot (active) and wet (passive). Its property in the world of creation is to rarefy and render things finer, lighter, more delicate, softer, and consequently better able to move to the higher spheres.

The Qualities of Fire are Hot and Dry

Fire is naturally hot (active) and dry (passive) and similar to air, it rarefies, refines, and intermingles with all things. However, it is its penetrative power that enables it to traverse the substance of the air. With this power it subsumes the coldness of the two heavy cold elements as well. By this power it brings the elementary properties into harmony.

The Qualities of Water are Cold and Wet

The nature of water is cold (active) and wet (passive). It appears to our senses as long as there are no influences to counteract it. It lends itself readily to dispersion and therefore assumes any shape without permanency.

The Qualities of Earth are Cold and Dry

Earth is naturally cold (active) and dry (passive). These qualities of the earth can be easily appreciated by our senses as long as there is no interference by extraneous agents and it obeys its particular nature. It is by means of the element of earth that the parts of our body are fixed and held together into a compacted form. This is how our outward form is maintained.

***

When the two passive qualities (dry and wet) are balanced, the degree of heat will come to a limit. It will never be predominant, for that would lead to dryness. If dryness is associated with the heat, the imbalanced temperament may be maintained over a long period of time whereas if the heat is associated with moistness, the imbalanced temperament will be of short duration because the moisture becomes predominant and obliterates the heat. However, the heat sometimes comes to predominate and obliterate the moisture, producing dryness.

Moisture allows shapes to be readily created from it while dryness, on the other hand, permits forms to be assumed only with difficulty and they are resolved with similar difficulty. When dryness and moisture alternate, dryness is overruled by the moisture, and thus the object is easily susceptible of being molded into a form whereas if the moisture were overruled by dryness, the form and features of the body would become firm and constant. Moisture serves to protect dryness from friability. Dryness prevents moisture from dispersing.

Every living thing is composed of these elemental qualities of hot, cold, wet and dry. Within we humans, animals and plants, the humours function contain the elemental qualities of hot, cold, wet and dry.

CHAPTER 2

The Humours

THE NATURE OF HUMOURS

UNDERSTANDING THE FOUR ELEMENTS THROUGH their particular functions, we know that according to Avicenna Cuisine, our humours are generated by our process of digestion of food and drink that we consume that are transformed into the humours in our liver. They are fluids which flow within us and nourish our bodies. Healthy humours depend on our diet and the foods and drinks that we consume in addition to how we prepare them. The humours convert our food and drink into our nourishment. Based on Avicenna's work, we know that the food we eat is responsible for nourishing our tissues, energizing our metabolism, giving up our needed energy to survive, creating wastes that have to be evacuated and, finally, determines our state of good or ill health as we will show with specific examples in this guidebook.

THE FOUR TYPES OF HUMOURS

The normal humours are of the following four types: blood humour, yellow bile humour, phlegmatic humour and black bile humour.

THE BLOOD HUMOUR (AIR)

The nature and dynamic aspect of the blood humour is hot and wet just as elemental air. It may be normal or abnormal, conforming to its nature or not. Normal blood is red in color, sweet in taste and free from smell.

THE YELLOW BILE HUMOUR (FIRE)

The yellow bile humour is the foam of our blood and is considered hot and dry similar to elemental fire. It is bright in color and is also light and pungent. The more red it is, the hotter it is. Yellow bile is formed in the liver and then follows one of two courses: either it circulates with the blood or it passes on to the gallbladder.

The part that passes into the blood stream assists in two purposes. First of all, the portion that goes to the blood is essential for nourishing organs like the lungs. It makes the blood light and thin for easy passage through the narrow channels of the body. The portion that goes into the gallbladder is thus prevented from causing the body to become faulty and providing nutrition to the gallbladder. Yellow bile's subsidiary functions are the cleansing of the intestine from the thick and sticky mucus and stimulation of the muscles of the intestine and rectum for proper defecation.

THE PHLEGMATIC HUMOUR (WATER)

The nature of the phlegmatic humour is cold and wet just like the element of water. Normal (sweet) phlegmatic humour can be transformed into blood at anytime, as it is an imperfectly matured blood. Phlegm is a kind of sweet fluid that is only slightly colder than the body, but is much colder than the yellow bile and blood humours.

THE BLACK BILE HUMOUR (EARTH)

The black bile humour is cold and dry in nature similar to elemental earth. Normal black bile is a sediment of normal blood. It has a taste between sweetness and bitterness. After being formed in the liver, a part goes to the blood and another to the spleen. The part that goes with the blood is essential for two purposes: the nutrition of organs such as the bones that have an appreciable quantity of the black bile in their composition, and to make the blood properly thick and heavy. The portion that is in excess of these requirements is taken up by the spleen, essentially for its own nutrition, but also to save the blood from being damaged. The portion that goes from the spleen into the stomach serves the purpose of making the stomach strong and firm. It also stimulates the appetite because of its sour taste.

This action of the black bile humour is somewhat similar to that of the yellow bile humour, both of them being known as "bile," yellow or black. Just as the surplus of bile in the blood goes to the gallbladder, and the surplus from the gallbladder passes into the intestine, the excess of black bile humour from the blood goes to the spleen. What is left over from the spleen goes to the stomach to induce appetite. It is significant to note that while the surplus of yellow bile humour excites peristaltic movements and thus assists evacuation, the surplus of black bile humour encourages the intake of food.

***

It is our humours that hold our temperaments in balance as the humours provide the energy for our temperament and they each share the same elemental qualities.

CHAPTER 3

The Temperaments

OUR TEMPERAMENT, CREATED BY THE HUMOURS, through the digestive process, combines our physical and mental characteristics as well as our emotional and spiritual qualities. Our inherent temperament depends upon our parents' temperament, time and place of our birth, our age and the climate in which we were born, among other considerations. However, it may change through our nurturing process. As a result, each one of us is an individual with different characteristics and qualities. Our temperament has a direct relationship with our health and well being. If we each know our temperament, we can plan a diet that best suits each one of us.

As Avicenna says, temperament is the quality that results from the mutual interaction of the four contrary, primary qualities of elements within the humours, namely, hot, cold, wet and dry. By dividing up into minute particles, the elemental qualities are able to secure contact among themselves. These qualities are so minutely intermingled as each to lie in very close relationship to one another. Their opposite powers alternately conquer and become conquered until a state of equilibrium is reached which is uniform throughout the whole. It is this outcome that is called "the temperament."

Since the primary energies in the elemental qualities are four in number (namely: heat, cold, moisture, dryness), it is evident that the temperaments in bodies undergoing generation and destruction accord with these qualities.

A simple, rational classification is of two types: (a) Balanced. Here the contrary qualities are present to exactly equal degrees of potency—neither of them being in excess or deficiency. This temperament has a quality that is exactly the mean between the two extremes. (b) Imbalanced. Here the quality of the temperament is not an exquisitely exact mean between the two contraries, but tends a little more to one than to the other. For example, too hot more than too cold; too moist more than too dry and so on.

It is to be noted that a temperament is never strictly balanced or strictly imbalanced. A perfectly balanced temperament does not actually exist in the human being any more than it exists in any of our organs. Moreover, the term balanced does not refer to weight but to an equity of distribution. It is this distribution, which is the primary consideration—whether we are referring to our body as a whole, or only to some individual organ. The average measure of these as to quantity and quality, is that which standard human nature ought to have—both in terms of the best proportion and in equity of distribution. As a matter of fact, the mean between excess and deficiency of qualities, such as is characteristic of we humans, actually is very close to the theoretical ideal as opposed to that of other animals or plants.

CHAPTER 4

Physiology

INTRODUCTION

IN ORDER FOR OUR BODY TO SURVIVE, we need the power to animate or invigorate our "self." We have to be able to receive nutrition, grow and continuously restore or regenerate our body and be able to procreate our human species for the purpose of its continuation. In addition, we need to be conscious and aware of our environment for the purpose of self-preservation.

These functions according to Avicenna, are known as the Vital, Natural and Neural energies, each relate to a specific organ or organs in our body. Our Vital Energy is located in our heart, our Natural Energy in our liver and male and female reproductive organs; and our Neural Energy in our brain.

THE THREE BASIC DRIVES

VITAL ENERGY (HEART)

Our Vital Energy resembles our Natural Energy in that its actions are beyond the scope of the will. It resembles our Neural Energy in carrying out contrary actions in that it expands or dilates and contracts at one and the same time effecting two contrary movements at once. According to Avicenna, our Vital Energy is the power that the organs receive before they can accomplish various functions of our living being.

Scientists in the past have claimed that this energy, besides paving the way for "life," itself initiates the movement of the Breath of Life that is towards the various organs and is the agent that brings about the contraction and expansion of respiration and pulse. When it assists life, it is "passive." When it assists the activity and functions of the mind and pulse, it is "active" by preserving the integrity of the Breath of Life.

Natural Energy (Liver)

Our Natural Energy is responsible for two things. First, the preservation of our individual self and our nutrition and growth. This energy is located in the liver, where its functions emerge. Secondly, the Natural Energy is responsible for the reproductive power that pertains to the generation and preservation of the race. More specifically, our sexual functions like the formation of germinal fluid and its fertilization of the ovum into the specific form. This energy is also located in the generative organs and its functions proceed from them.

Neural Energy (Brain)

Our Neural Energy consists of our abilities of sensation/perception and movement/motivation. Our sensation/perception functions contain (1) five external senses (seeing, hearing, tasting, touching and smelling) and five internal senses (common sense, retention, imagination, estimation and memory). Our movement/motivation abilities operate our (2) physical movement and neural motivation. Neural motivation includes the concupiscent function (attraction to pleasure or motivation for food and sex to preserve our species) and irascible function (avoidance of pain by defending and preserving our individual self).

CHAPTER 5

The Breath of Life and Innate
Heat as Energy Givers

OUR BREATH ACTS AS THE LINK BETWEEN OUR BODY, mind (soul) and energy (spirit). It is the breath that makes the perfect equilibrium of the elements, humours and temperament possible. The first breath is from our Vital Energy, hot and dry. According to Avicenna, it has its center in the left ventricle of the heart, preserves life, causes the body to grow, move and reproduce, and travels through the arteries. It actualizes the potential energy of our Vital Energy.

Avicenna says that the left side of the heart is hollow so that it can serve both as a storehouse of the breath and as the seat of manufacture of the breath. Our breath also enables the energies of our physiological network to be conveyed into the corresponding organs. Our breath is the rallying-point for our energy. It is as an emanation into the various organs and tissues of our body whereby these are then able to actualize the functions of those energies. The energies of the various organs are actualized by our Vital Energy that provides our body with its Innate Heat.

Within our body, there are dense structures such as our organs and their various tissues which are formed with the heavier portions of our humors of the corresponding temperament. Our "breath" or Vital Energy, however, is formed through the light and vapory part of the humors of the corresponding temperament and our Innate Heat.

As soon as our breath and appropriate temperament meet, our Vital Energy is actualized. During this time, all the members are rendered capable of receiving all the other energies—sensation and otherwise. Our sensation/perception ability does not appear in our breath and organs until our Vital Energy has come into being. Even if our sensation/perception abilities in a given organ are lost, our life will remain in the part until our Vital Energy has forsaken it.

Our Vital Energy is that which appears in our breath at the very moment when our breath develops out of the less dense particles of the humors. When a particular portion of our breath reaches the appropriate parts of our brain, it becomes impressed with the temperament of the brain. It thereby adapts itself for the operations of the energies that proceed from and remain in it. The same applies in the case of the liver and reproductive organs.

***

    The beginning of our breath is a natural emanation from potentiality to actuality proceeding without intermission until its form (preparation, state) is completed and perfected. Each organ, though derived from the self-same substance as the humours, nevertheless has its own particular temperament—for the proportional qualities of the denser portions of our humours and the form of their commixture are peculiar to each organ.

CHAPTER 6

The Organs

EVERY ANIMAL AND EVERY ONE OF ITS ORGANS develops the most appropriate and the best adapted temperament for its various functions and passive states. We humans have been bestowed a most befitting temperament and most appropriate energies for the various active and passive states in our body. Similarly, every organ and member is endowed with the proper temperament appropriate to its own functional requirement. Some are more hot, others more cold, others drier and others wetter.

THE HOT-TEMPERED ORGANS

The Breath of Life and our heart, which is the center of Vital Energy, are the hottest in the body. Next is our blood that, although produced in the liver, due to its contact with our heart, is hotter than our liver. The next is our liver that is really a mass of almost solidified blood. After this is our flesh that is colder than our liver due to the cold nervous tissue in it. The next is our muscles which, due to their cold ligaments and tendons, are not as hot as our flesh. After this comes our spleen that, due to its high content of the residue from broken up blood, is not as hot. Our kidneys are less hot because they have only a little blood. Then there are our breasts, testicles and muscular coats of the arteries that are warm as they contain hot blood and other vital fluids. The next in order are our veins, which are slightly warmer because of blood in them. Last is the skin of the palm of our hand, which is evenly balanced.

THE COLD-TEMPERED ORGANS

The coldest thing in our body is phlegm. Then, in order of coldness, are our hair, bones, cartilage, ligaments, phlegmatic membranes, nerves, spinal cord, brain, solid and liquid fats, and lastly our skin.

THE WET-TEMPERED ORGANS

The primary temperament of an organ is always similar to that of its nutriment, while its secondary temperament is determined by its excrement. The lungs, as Galen himself stated, are nourished by our hot blood that contains an appreciable quantity of yellow bile humour. If our lungs are moist, it is because of the vapors from below and the catarrhal secretions from above. Our liver is more moist than our lungs due to its intrinsic moisture, while our lungs appear to be moist because of its extrinsic moisture. As they are constantly soaked in the extrinsic moisture or secretions, this makes them structurally even in level of moistness.

The same is similar in regards to phlegm and blood. The moisture in phlegm is of a kind that merely moistens our tissues, while the moisture in our blood is of such a type that it is integrated into the very structure of our organs. Although normally there is more moisture in phlegm than in blood, in the maturation of phlegm into blood, it becomes dispersed because normal phlegm is nothing but imperfectly digested blood.

THE DRY-TEMPERED ORGANS

Our hair is the driest of the tissues. It is, as it were, solid residue from the evaporation of moisture. Next in order are our bones, which due to dryness are the hardest of organs. Our bones are, however, a little bit more moist than our hair. Our bones are formed from blood. They are constantly absorbing moisture from the attached muscles. They dry up the humours naturally located in bones. Next in order of dryness are cartilage, ligaments tendons, membranes, arteries, veins, motor nerves, heart, sensory nerves and our skin. Motor nerves are colder and drier at the same time and are therefore in balance.

CHAPTER 7

The Digestive Assistant Drives

THE DRIVES PERTAINING TO THE PRESERVATION OF THE LIFE OF THE INDIVIDUAL

NUTRITION ALTERS THE FOOD IN SUCH A WAY that it becomes temperamentally similar to our body, and is thus rendered suitable for the repair of daily wear and tear of our tissues. The power of growth develops our organs in their appropriate spatial relationships and integrates our nutritive material according to the requirements of the individual growth.

Nutrition serves our Natural Energy to grow by providing the necessary nutriment. Sometimes the quantity of nutriment may be sufficient only for the day-to-day needs of repair, but at times it may be more or less than the daily requirements. Growth, for instance, is only possible when the quantity of nutriment is in excess of the actual requirements.

THE DRIVES ASSISTING DIGESTION

With the Natural Energy, the real assisting drives are the various processes that assist nutrition, which are fourfold: attraction, digestion (fermenting action of our body), retention and elimination.

ATTRACTION

Our attraction assistant to the digestive process draws suitable or apparently suitable material inside our body for nutrition. It is served by longitudinal fibers. The liver attracts the chyme from our stomach and then sends the purer parts out through the veins.

DIGESTION

Our digestive assistant transmutes the material from its former state until it works up into a temperament which enables it to become efficient nutrient material. This process is "digestion" in the strict sense. At the same time, it produces a change in the superfluities so that they can be easily discharged from the organ containing them. This process is called "maturation" (that is, the liquefaction of the waste products for proper elimination).

RETENTION

The retentive process retains the food while the alterative (transformative) power is engaged in preparing sound nutritive substances from it. It generally acts through the oblique but sometimes also through the transverse fibers.

EVACUATION/ELIMINATION

The eliminative process is concerned with the elimination of the non-nutritive excremental matters that are left over from our digestion of food as well as the nutritive material taken in excess of nutritional requirements and the material which, having served its purpose, is no longer required like water which is eliminated in urine. Our waste matter is expelled through the natural channels or meridians of excretion, that is, the urinary tract for the excretion of urine and large intestine for the elimination of feces. When, however, these routes are not available, waste matter is diverted either from a superior to an inferior organ or from a hard organ to a soft one.

COMPARATIVE RELATIONS BETWEEN THE QUALITIES AND THE DRIVES

If we compare the degree of active (heat, cold) and passive (dry, wet) qualities needed for our various powers, we find that the retentive assistant needs more dryness than heat. This is because more time is required for a movement to come to rest than is needed to start the transverse fibers to move in contraction.

INTERRELATION BETWEEN
THE QUALITIES AND THE POWERS

Our four digestive assistants are served by the four elemental qualities—hot, cold, wet and dry. Heat is the underlying factor in all these assistant drives.

HOT

Heat is necessary for movement and it takes only a short time to produce its effect so that the remainder of the time is occupied in holding the material and coming to a state of rest.

The attractive assistant needs more heat than dryness because the main feature of attraction is movement and movement needs heat. The organs concerned must move rather than be at rest and contracted which requires dryness. This power, however, does not require much movement, although at times vigorous activity becomes necessary. (1) Attraction is brought about by an attractive power—as when a magnet attracts iron; (2) and by heat as when oil is drawn up in a lamp. Heat increases the power of attraction exerted by the power of the attraction assistant.

The digestive process requires more heat than the other three assistants. Hence, the reason why we should exercise before we eat is to create heat and allow our body to properly digest our foods and drinks.

DRY

The action of dryness is directly instrumental in the functions of two powers—digestion and retention. It is secondary and auxiliary in the case of the other two—attraction and expulsion. Dryness helps the retentive assistant because it favors muscular contraction upon the contents of the organ. The digestive power needs moisture and not dryness. The action of moisture, on the other hand, hinders strong and free movement by unduly relaxing the fibers. Dryness serves the retentive process by increasing the contractility of the fibers. This is, however, of little use to digestion.

COLD

The action of cold serves all four assistants. All the assistants act by virtue of movement, which is shown not only as attraction and expulsion, but even in the digestion proper. Movement is also concerned indirectly with the retentive assistant because the transverse muscular fibers come into play. Coldness weakens and hinders this assistant in all its functions, yet indirectly it helps it by fixing the fibers in the position referred to. Therefore it is not directly concerned with the assistant's abilities. It simply causes their instruments to be in a state that will help to maintain their functions.

Cold helps expulsion: (1) by increasing the density of gases; (2) by keeping the particles of the digested material as coarse; (3) and by its astringent action upon the transverse muscular fibers. This action, being preparatory, may be regarded as an indirect help. In short, cold helps the assistants indirectly. If it had been concerned directly, there would have been no movement at all and the real purpose would have been completely defeated.

Wet

The digestive drive does not need dryness. It needs moisture. The nutrients are rendered fluid with moisture. The nutrients are then able to enter the pores. They are molded to conform with the channels or meridians to be traversed. But we must not assume that because moisture aids digestion, children, whose temperament is moist, can digest hard or indigestible foods. This can be done in youth, but here the reason is not to be found in their moisture. It is because at that period of life, their nature is similar to that of the foods in question. Foods of a hard nature are not appropriate for the temperament of children. Therefore, their digestive power cannot cope with such foods. Their retentive drive cannot tolerate it. Their expulsive drive rapidly expels it. In the case of young people, on the other hand, hard food is quite suitable for nourishment.

Therefore, our attractive assistant has a quite short duration of muscular contraction and a marked amount of longitudinal movement achieved. Our digestive assistant has a continued duration of muscular contraction and no amount of longitudinal movement achieved. Our retentive assistant has a long, continued duration of muscular contraction and a moderate amount of longitudinal movement achieved. Our expulsive assistant has a momentary duration of muscular contraction and a considerable, but super added from without, amount of longitudinal movement achieved. Therefore the various drives make use of these four assistants in diverse ways and to different extents.

Part II

The Six Nurturing Essentials

The important nurturing essentials in the world around us that affect our humours and, thereby, our temperament are called the Six Nurturing Essentials. It is possible that one or more of these will negatively impact our temperament. As an example, if we are among those who have a Fiery (hot and dry) temperament, we will be affected by an excess of heat and dryness. These would include eating an excessive amount of hot and dry foods, undertaking excessive exercise or having an angry outburst. These overheat our body. Being aware of the effects of the Six Nurturing Essentials will help us to maintain a healthy lifestyle.

CHAPTER 8

Air and the Environment

WHERE WE LIVE UNDENIABLY HAS AN IMPACT on our health. Think about the world's geography, seasonal and climate changes, and all the environmental factors. These all come into play when determining our health status, especially when it comes to the art of breathing, which is the basis of all public health and environmental medicine.

Air is a fundamental constituent of our physical body and its Vital Energy. Through its constant supply, our Vital Energy is kept actively conditioned. Air is the agent that modifies our breath, not simply as an element, but by virtue of its constructive and regulatory nature.

When we first draw air in, it necessarily cools our breath, but after the air attains the quality of our breath, through continued contact with its heat, it stops being a modifier, and becomes excessive. Therefore, new air is needed and when we breathe in, it supplies the place of the other. We must evacuate the old air in order to give place for the new, and, at the same time, remove with it the excessive energies from the substance of our breath.

As long as the air's temperament is modified and pure and has no substances mixed in which would oppose the temperament of our breath, health will come and remain. Otherwise the opposite occurs.

FRESH AIR

Our bodies require fresh air that is free from pollution, smoke and vapor and is available in the open rather than in enclosed or covered places. Open air is the best, but when the outside air becomes polluted, the inside air is rather preferable. The best air is that which is pure, clean and free from contamination with vapors from lakes, trenches, bamboo fields, saline affected areas and vegetable fields.

It is also essential that the air we breathe should be open to the fresh breeze and not enclosed. Fresh air comes from the plains and high mountains. It is not confined in pits and depressions, hence it is quickly warmed by the rising sun and cools after the sunset. Air is not fresh if it is enclosed within recently painted or plastered walls. Fresh air also does not produce any choking or discomfort.

THE INFLUENCE OF THE SEASONS ON OUR BODY

Seasonal changes have a far-reaching effect on our body. This is, however, not due to any time relationship as such, but to the qualitative change in the season. It is for this reason that heat and cold produce different effects on different individuals. For instance, it is best that the autumn should have rains and the winter should be milder rather than severe or altogether absent. Similarly, the spring should be rainy and the summer not absolutely dry.

THE CHANGES THAT SPRING PRODUCES IN OUR BODY

During the spring, illnesses can tend to be activated due to the movement of our humours that had been lying dormant during the winter. This is the reason why if we are Earthy-tempered (cold and dry or melancholic) individuals, we may become agitated in this season. Those of us who have an excess of humours may suffer from illnesses caused by the liquidation and mixing up of the humours. When the spring becomes prolonged, there is a significant reduction in our having summer illnesses. In relation to the periods of life, spring is especially wholesome for children and adolescents.

THE CHANGES THAT SUMMER PRODUCES IN OUR BODY

The summer disperses our humours and Vital Energy and either weakens them or increases their functions. Blood, one of our four humours, tends to decrease in quantity while bile, another humour, tends to increase. Towards the end of the summer, there is a predominance of black bile as the thinner parts of our humours are dispersed, leaving the heavier parts behind.

THE CHANGES THAT AUTUMN PRODUCES IN OUR BODY

During the autumn season, illness tends to be greater. This is due to: (1) the hot sun during the day and cold during the night, which produces wide fluctuations of temperature in our body. (2) Excessive consumption of fruit causes an imbalance of the humours. In addition, bad articles of our diet causes weakened matter to spread and leave dense particles behind, which then undergo oxidation. (3) The fermenting humours pass to the skin in the summer. In the autumn season, the cold atmosphere causes the humours to be thrown back into the interior parts where they accumulate and are, as it were, imprisoned. (4) The energy of our body is impaired from the effects of the prior summer continuing into this season.

In relation to periods of life, the first part of autumn is to some extent beneficial to the elderly, but the last part of autumn is very injurious to them because there is cold and because there is the residue of oxidation of humours from the summer season.

THE CHANGES THAT WINTER PRODUCES IN OUR BODY

The winter is particularly beneficial to the digestive process because: (1) Due to cold, our Vital Energy is enclosed in our body and thus becomes stronger and less prone to dispersion. (2) There is less fruit consumed during the winter. (3) There is less movement and activity after meals. (4) There is a greater tendency to remain in warm places.

CHAPTER 9

Physical Rest and Activity

IT IS ESSENTIAL THAT WE FIND THE RIGHT balance between exercise and rest. Think about how to design a safe, effective, sensible and appropriate exercise routine and regimen that is right for you. Learning the value of proper exercise is vital and can be unique for every individual.

The effect of exercise on the human body varies according to its degree—mild or severe, the amount of rest taken, and the movement of the associated humors.

The effect of movement on our human body depends on whether the movement is vigorous or mild, whether it is prolonged or moderate, whether it is accompanied by rest, and whether it is controlled by matter (like fire with firefighter or water with the Olympic swimmers). All kinds of movements, whether vigorous, or prolonged or short, or accompanied by rest, act together in stirring heat. But the short vigorous movement differs from the prolonged non-vigorous movement and from the prolonged movement accompanied by rest. This is because short vigorous movements make our bodies very hot and cause less dispersion, if at all, whereas prolonged movement, even if mild, produces greater dispersion than warming. When either of the two—short vigorous movement or prolonged non-vigorous movement—is excessive, it produces coldness, because it excessively disperses our Innate Heat and also dilutes it.

When our movement is controlled by our humours, it may sometimes become strong and sometimes weak. For instance, if it is the movement involved in an Olympic swimmers occupation, it is liable to produce cold and moisture, whereas if it is the movement involved in a firefighter's occupation, it is liable to produce more heat and dryness. As for rest, it is always cooling because there is no excitation of heat and there is congestion, which soothes the heat. Moreover, rest is moistening because there is no dispersion of our excessive energies.

The value of exercise includes the following: (1) It hardens the organs and renders them fit for their functions. (2) It results in a better absorption of food, aids assimilation, and, by increasing the Innate Heat, improves nutrition. (3) It clears the pores of the skin. (4) It removes effete substances through the lungs. (5) It strengthens the physique. Vigorous exercise invigorates the muscular and nervous system.

Exercise and heating agents set in motion the blood (Air) humor, the yellow bile (Fire) humour, and even the black bile (Earth) humor (which is thereby strengthened). Rest sets the phlegmatic (Water) humor in motion and strengthens it. Rest also strengthens some kinds of black bile (Earth) humor. Even imagination, emotional states and other agents cause the humors to move.

THE TIME FOR EXERCISE

The best time to exercise is when the body is free from impurities in the internal organs and blood vessels so that there is no risk of unhealthy chyme being dispersed through the body by the exercise. Yesterday's food should have passed both gastric and hepatic digestion, and also intravascular digestion—the time when our next meal is soon approaching, which can be ascertained by examining the urine as to its substance and color.

If it is some time before the next meal is due, and there is a need for more nutriment, and the urine is high-colored, this indicates that exercise at this time would be detrimental, namely by exhausting our strength. For this reason, Avicenna says that when vigorous exercise takes place, it is best that the stomach is not empty. There should still be a little bit more food in the stomach in the winter, and a little bit less in the summer. Moreover, it is better to choose a time for exercise when we are not hungry, and when we are hot and moist rather than cold and dry. The best time is actually between the two. Individuals with a hot and dry temperament who exercise may be more prone to illness and benefit from avoiding vigorous exercises.

It is important that a person who is about to exercise should first get rid of the effete matters of the body by way of the intestines and bladder. In the spring the best time for exercise is around midday and should be done in a moderately warm room. In summer, the exercise should be done earlier. In winter, it should be delayed until evening, but there are other objections to doing so. Consequently, in winter, the location of exercise should be moderately warm, to enable exercise to be carried out at a time when the aliment is digested and the effete matters have been expelled.

CHAPTER 10

Sleep and Wakefulness

EVERY INDIVIDUAL SHOULD LEARN TO DESIGN a healthful daily routine that balances adequate, sound and restful sleep with appropriate, constructive wakeful activity. It is important to harmonize our personal sleep and wake cycles with the rhythms of nature.

Sleep strengthens our natural assisting drives (the digestion of food and elaboration of the digestive products into good humours) by enclosing our Innate Heat within our body and relaxing our senses, which are asleep. It does so because it moistens and relaxes the channels of our breath.

Sleep removes all types of lethargy and it prevents strong evacuations. If it is then followed by appropriate exercise, it strengthens our body. Sleep induces sweating. When we sweat heavily during sleep, without obvious cause, nutrients have accumulated in excess of our bodily requirements. When sleep encounters matter adapted for digestion and maturation, it turns it into the nature of blood and warms it. As a result, our Innate Heat is stimulated, travels through, and warms our whole body. If there are hot yellow bile humours and the period of sleep is prolonged, there is an abnormal production of heat.

Sleeping on an empty stomach produces more dispersion than coldness in our body. During sleep, the indigestible foods, being partially digested, tend to produce coldness. Wakefulness has quite the opposite affect. When wakefulness is excessively prolonged, it produces disturbances of the brain such as dryness, weakness and impairment of our Neural Energy and its intellectual functions.

Wakefulness is, however the contrary in all these respects. Excessive wakefulness oxidizes the humours and produces hot types of illnesses. Excess sleep, on the other hand, dulls the nervous and Neural Energy and its intellectual functions and makes our head heavy. Due to lack of dispersion, cold types of illnesses also follow.

Wakefulness increases our desire for food and stimulates our appetite by dispersing our body's wastes. It however, impairs our digestion by dispersing our Natural Energy.

A restless and disturbed sleep (insomnia), being in a state between wakefulness and sleep, is bad for all our bodily states. Lack of sleep entails an imprisonment of our Innate Heat and causes our body to become cold exteriorly. This is why warm blankets are needed to keep our limbs and entire body warm during sleep, which is not required in our waking state.

CHAPTER 11

Emotions and Aromatherapy

PSYCHOLOGICAL EMOTIONS ARE THE NEXT ESSENTIAL factor that determines our health and well being. Our mental and emotional states have a tremendous impact on the health and management of our temperament, mind and our emotions. Each emotion that we have will create a differing qualitative effect upon our body. By recognizing these, we go a long way in controlling our health.

According to Avicenna Cuisine, emotions also have temperaments. For instance, anger is hot and dry or penetrating, functioning like the element fire, yellow bile humour and the Fiery temperament; depression is hot and wet or rarefying, functioning like the element air, the blood humour and the Airy temperament; grief is cold and dry or compacting, functions like the element earth, the black bile humour and the Earthy temperament; fear is cold and wet or dispersing, functioning like the element water, phlegmatic humour and the Watery temperament.

VARIOUS EMOTIONAL STATES AND OUR BREATH

Joy and sadness, fear and anger are passions that are peculiarly related to the breath in our heart.

JOY AND THE CAUSE OF HAPPINESS

Happiness implies attaining a goal, and when we succeed, it can only cause us to be happy because we are aware of a change for the good. Joy is a form of happiness. We are happy when a corresponding energy within us is joyful. For instance, we may taste something sweet or flavorful or smell a pleasant fragrance, or overcome a feeling of anger with good judgment or realize some useful outcome of our reasoning or imagination. There is a certain power accruing from every perfect level of happiness. It is the perfection of the given energy that produces joy.

THE EFFECT OF QUANTITY OF THE BREATH

If our breath has an abundant tendency to encompass happiness, its action will be correspondingly powerful. The greater its force, the greater the amount will persist at the place of its origin—that is, in its "matrix." Consequently, under these circumstances it will radiate out in greater measure to our various organs and produce that particular state of expansion that spells joy and pleasure. If our breath were only moderate in amount, the substrate concerned would hold it greedily and not allow it to expand as freely as otherwise would be the case. A person with asthma who constantly feels wheezy may relate to this theory from Avicenna in that the lack of air going into the lungs causes grief and the inability to experience joy to its fullest extent.

THE EFFECT OF THE QUALITY OF THE BREATH

The more noble the character possessed by air and the more noble its substance, the more luminous it becomes and the more celestial the substance will be. This can rationalize various points about quality and air and our tendency towards pleasure and joy.

In regards to sorrow and grief, it is just a question of the opposite. Once the general sources of happiness and pleasure are thoroughly grasped, the sources of joy become understandable, since joy is a form of delight.

By way of summary, it may be said that when the breath that resides in our heart is plentiful, when it is balanced in temperament, when it has a luminous, beautiful and is a bright substance, then, we have a strong tendency to be joyful.

When our breath is scanty, when it is not balanced in temperament, and when it is: (a) very dense and coarse in substance (as in melancholic and elderly people), it cannot arouse joy; (b) very delicate in substance (as in convalescents), it will not allow expansion; and (c) confused (as in melancholic-tempered people). In all these cases there is a very strong tendency to depression, sadness and grief.

How Each Emotion Tends to Generate
its Own Type of Breath

It is not to be thought that every agent tending towards joy or depression necessarily depends only on the quantity or quality of the substance of our breath. Other agencies are also concerned. For instance, the emotions of our mind have to be considered. These tend to one or other of the previously mentioned, true though it be that they act through the agency of factors internal in our breath itself (namely, quantity, quality). They do this by modifying our temperamental substrate, or by rectifying our breath, or by increasing its quantity. Thus, we become joyful. On the other hand, an agent of the opposite sign will tend to induce depression. These are the immediate and remote, external factors.

The internal factors are traceable to one single source, because every act of contrary type, if it were repeated often, comes to be more efficient in imparting an effect. Every increment of power carries with it so much more tendency to the accomplishment of the effect. This is sufficiently plain from a purely logical point of view. A body that is very heating tends to impart heat rapidly; and similarly—in the case of cold, rare and dense bodies. The same holds good in the case of the internal potencies. This is how it is when a strong character is formed by repeated practice and repeated experience of emotion. It is in this way that moral character is acquired.

Perhaps the reason underlying this is that when an emotion appears, it often makes the substance of the breath become conducive and what is suitable for one thing is unsuitable for its opposite. The more often it is repeated, the less the tendency to the opposite becomes, for that which is conducive to the opposite, is expelled little by little. This is saying the same thing as logic says. It emerges when a repeat of being happy disposes our breath to a state of gladness. A repeat of being sad disposes us to depression.

The strengthening of our Natural Drive is contributed to by three factors, each of which is itself a source of gladness; (a) the temperament of our breath; (b) the overproduction of our breath beyond that which is lost by dispersal; and (c) the prevention of excessive dispersal of our breath. Our breath becoming less dense is followed by two things: a tendency towards movement and expansion—this is related to the thinness of its substance; and an attraction to itself of its own particular nutriment.

This is due to the movement of expansion towards a place away from the movement of the nutriment. This particular attraction is really the natural physical tendency to avoid emptiness. In its essence, it is the same with any movement that in itself brings it to pass. What is there is replaced by what comes after. It is the outcome of this law that very distant waters are drawn towards their primary source and that winds follow the course they do.

Two things follow great depression: the weakening of our Natural Energy and the concentration of our breath. The explanation of this is that violent condensation and aggregation of our breath obliterates our Innate Heat and results in coldness.

It is therefore evident that intense happiness disposes our breath to gladness, while sadness disposes our breath to depression. The associated depressants do not make an impression on happiness unless they are vigorous.

How the Appropriate Aromas Stimulate and Strengthen the Breath

We now learn how the appropriate aromas can be stimulants and strengthen our breathing. Wine, for instance, restores our breath by nourishing it. Emblic Myrobalan, Amber and Coral concentrate our breath or prevent it from rapidly dissipating. Leopard's Bane modifies the temperament of our breath by giving it heat. Camphor and Rose Water do so by imparting cold. Sweet aromatics strengthen our breath by endowing its substance with agreeable and sweet fragrance. Dyer's Bugloss and Lapis Lazuli act by separating off black bile and fumes. Adding or removing an ingredient in the incense produces changes. For example, Coral may be joined with Amber and Dyer's Bugloss.

In some cases, happiness is the outcome of the intrinsic property of the aromatic. This is so in the case of Nard. In other cases, the intrinsic property of the food produces its effect indirectly by acting upon one or other of the primary causes of gladness. Thus, Musk and Amber act on our breath by way of their aromatic quality. Apple Juice gives rise to happiness by virtue of an intrinsic property. But when used in a case where the temperament of the breath is hot, the stimulant action is effected by way of cooling. When the temperament of the breath is cold, Leopard's Bane acts as stimulant both by virtue of its intrinsic property and by imparting warmth to the breath.

In dealing with all these aromas, then, it is necessary to know whether the properties are general or specific. When the property is general there is no need to make any modifications in employing it for a weak heart or depression. An instance of such an agent is afforded by the aromatic quality. On the other hand, where the property is specific, it requires modification. For instance, Apple Juice or Cider is cold and will stimulate one kind of temperament but not another. If one desires to use Apple Juice or Cider to make a cold-tempered person happy, it is necessary to counteract its coldness with a heating agent. It would be more efficient to choose a heating food, which itself is intrinsically a stimulant. For instance, Cinnamon or Nutmeg mixed with Apple Juice, because they supply both warmth and stimulating power.

Aromatic quality and sweetness are potencies that, though opposite, are yet attracted towards qualities that are agreeable to the substance of our breath. They supply the taste and fragrance that the Natural and Vital energies respectively desire to receive.

Where two aromas are of equal power, the sweeter and more aromatic of the two will prove a more efficient substance, because these properties are more attractive to the organs (especially the liver). Should nutrient properties be present as well, the breath is more rapidly nourished. Being healing in character, it acts more rapidly on the breath. These indications guide as to which aromas to use to obtain more rapid results.

The essence of an aromatic quality lies in its ability to thin or dilute. The essence of sweetness lies in its concentration and earthiness. This explains why aromatics are so much better adapted to feed our breath, while sweet substances are better fitted to nourish our body. Consequently an aromatic quality is more efficient for our heart than sweetness, while it is the other way round in the case of the liver. Our heart is the matrix of the generation of the nutriment of the breaths, whereas our liver is the matrix of generation of the nutriment of the body. That is why it needs less aromatic quality and more sweetness to nourish it than does our heart. All the same, an aromatic quality is required by our liver, because that organ is the matrix of our natural breath—not a matrix of generation of our breath, only a substrate for our breath to reside in.

Our natural breath has a desire for aromatics and is invigorated and refreshed by such. It is easy to see that the Natural Energy will also be invigorated.

CHAPTER 12

Retention and Evacuation

WE ALL NEED TO CONSTANTLY RECOGNIZE and cultivate the right balance between waste retention and waste evacuation. This means building healthy bowel habits and maintaining urinary health.

THE CAUSES OF RETENTION

The following are the causes of retention of our waste matters: (1) weak expulsive assistant drive: (a) a superabundance of waste matter so that our expulsive assistant drive cannot deal with it; and (b) insufficient informing sense for discharge of feces from our body, this act being aided by voluntary effort; and (2) unduly strong retentive assistant drive: (a) weakness of the digestive assistant so that food remains in our stomach too long and the natural retentive assistant drive holds the food back until it is sufficiently digested; (b) narrowness of the channels; and (c) their obstruction; (d) coarseness or viscidity of the waste matter.

THE CAUSES OF EVACUATION

The causes of our evacuation of matters that are normally retained include: (1) vigorous expulsive drive. (2) defective retentive assistant drive. (3) unfavorable quality of the matter that is (a) too heavy, because of a superabundant amount; (b) too distending owing to flatulent action; (c) corrosive and acrid in quality; and (d) attenuated of texture, making it too mobile and too easily expelled, and: (4) widening of the excretory channels. This occurs in the case of seminal flow.

The possible effects of evacuation of this type are: (1) Our temperament becomes cold because the substance is lost, which would otherwise increase that which maintains the Innate Heat. (2) Our temperament becomes hot if the evacuated material is cold in temperament like phlegmatic (serous) humor or mucus. (3) Our temperament becomes equable to blood if there is undue accumulation of the heating yellow bile humor so that the heat becomes superabundant. (4) Our temperament becomes dry. This is always intrinsic in origin. (5) Our temperament becomes moist in a matter analogous to that mentioned in regard to accidental increase in body heat, namely, either the evacuation of desiccant body fluid has not been too great or the Innate Heat is too scanty with the result that the aliment is not adequately digested and serous, phlegmatic humor becomes relatively increased. A moist temperament of this kind is unfavorable to the maintenance of our Innate Heat. Also, foreign heat will not serve as a substitute for our Innate Heat because of the difference of its nature.

The effect of excessive evacuations on the members of our body include: (1) coldness and dryness of their substance and nature ensue, even though they receive extraneous heat and moisture beyond their need; and (2) diseases from obstruction of the vessels due to undue dryness and narrowing of the veins.

When retention and evacuation are equally matched, and occur at the proper times, they are beneficial, and maintain health.

CHAPTER 13

Food, Diet, and Drink

INTRODUCTION

FOOD AND DRINK ARE THE EASIEST OF THE SIX nurturing essentials for us to control. Clearly, a lack of moderation by eating too much food or drinking too many liquids that are the same as our dominant temperament will have a negative impact on us.

There are three possibilities of how what we eat and drink can affect our body either by acting directly upon it or by its reaction to what we have consumed. Food and drink: (1) changed by our body but do not change our body because they are not assimilated and do not produce any nutrition; (2) changed by our body and produce a change in our body; and (3) not changed by our body, but itself produces changes in our body.

Another way of showing this is to say that food and drink act upon our body in three ways: (a) by the reaction of their elemental qualities of hot, cold, wet and dry alone without providing any nutritional value; (b) by the reaction of their elemental qualities of hot, cold, wet and dry providing nutritional value; or (c) by specific action of the food or drink consumed as a whole.

As these three possibilities are easily confused one with the other, they each require a precise definition. It is this way that we will be using them:

REACTION OF QUALITY ALONE

A food or drink becoming hot or cold when it enters our body is the reaction of our body to its elemental qualities of hot or cold. The food or drink we consume may produce heat or cold inside our body without providing any nutrition and without being assimilated.

REACTION OF ELEMENTAL QUALITIES AND NUTRITIONAL VALUE

When the nature of a food or drink (consisting of its elemental qualities) undergoes change and it adopts the form of any organ in our body, it may happen that by taking on the form of an organ in our body, the food or drink retains its original elemental qualities. These elemental qualities are stronger than those of our body. For example, blood produced from the digestion of lettuce remains colder than our body even after becoming blood and it is still suitable for becoming a part of any tissue in our body. In the same way, blood formed from the digestion of garlic continues to remain hot until it is fully utilized or destroyed in our body.

REACTION OF SPECIFIC ACTION OF A SUBSTANCE AS A WHOLE

This reaction is due to the specific nature and property of a food or drink and not to its elemental qualities. By quality we are referring to the four elemental qualities of hot, cold, wet and dry. A food or drink that acts through its own elemental quality does so independently of its nutritional value.

The nutritional value of a food or drink depends upon its ability to be digested and thereby nourish and strengthen the body by (1) repairing the organs and tissues that have been used up, (2) by increasing our Innate Heat through increasing our supply of blood, (3) or by acting through what remains of its original elemental quality.

However, by specific action we mean that which acts through a specific form that emerges after a temperament is formed by the elemental qualities. This occurs when there has been a mixing of the elemental qualities that gives rise to something that takes on a new form, over and above its elemental quality. This is neither a primary elemental quality nor the temperament that has arisen from the combining of the elements. It is rather the perfection that the elemental qualities take on from its temperament based on its capacity. Examples are the power of attraction of a magnet or the nature of the various types of plants and animals that emerge from the temperament based on the capacity of the temperament.

Therefore, specific form is neither the elemental qualities that make up the temperament of the food or drink nor the temperament itself. It is not hot, cold, wet or dry either separately or in combination, but it is like the individuality of a thing such as a color or a smell or some other form that we cannot perceive.

The specific form that appears after the temperament of the food or drink may be passive or active. An example of being passive would be brittleness. An example of being active would be sourness. When a property is active, it may or may not act upon our body. If it is does act upon our body, it may be a favorable or unfavorable action. In either case, this property is not due to its temperament, but to a specific property that it acquires after its temperament.

In regard to the qualitative action, when a food or drink is called hot or cold-tempered, this does not mean that it feels hot or cold-tempered to our body. What it means is that the food or drink has the potential to increase the heat or cold in our body. This can only occur when our Innate Heat acts upon it. It is only at that point that it becomes hot or cold to our body.

It may be that this quality is based upon a tendency within it such as when we say that sulfur is potentially hot. It may also be that when we say that a certain food or drink is hot or cold, we are referring to the heat or coldness of its temperament based on its elemental qualities without us referring to what action it takes in our body. Just as once we learned to write, this ability remains a potential within us.

The difference between a specific property and an action by the elemental qualities is that the action by the elemental qualities appears only after a food or drink has been metabolized in our body. A specific property, on the other hand, shows itself either all at once as with the venom from a snakebite or after some further action within our body as is the case with aconite.

Foods and drinks that are changed and metabolized by the body, but do not produce any change in our body are either (a) nutritive or (b) non-nutritive.

Foods and drinks that are changed by our body and also produce changes in the body are (a) those whose action ceases after the digestion and are either assimilated or not; (b) those whose action continues even after the digestion until they produce destructive changes in the body.

Foods and drinks that produces change in our body without changing themselves are known as the actual poisons.

Some nutrient foods are medicinal in quality rather than nutrients. Others are nutrients such as Wine, Egg Yolk, Meat Juice and so forth. Others are less so such as Bread and Pasta. Still others are entirely different to the nutrients of the blood and are only medicinal foods.

How the Quantity of Food and Drink Can Affect Our Body

Food affects our body not only in terms of its quality as we have seen, but also in terms of the quantity we consume.

We know that foods eaten in excessive amounts, beyond our normal requirements, produce a reaction in our body where our body becomes adverse to the food causing indigestion, constipation, obstructions and intestinal decay. We also know that foods eaten below what our body's daily requirements are, cause our body to begin to weaken, dry up and waste away. An increase in the amount of food we consume always has a cooling effect unless decomposition supervenes in our digestive system giving rise to heat. This heat, due to the change being caused by decay and decomposition of food, is extraneous. Changes in the extra nutriment are the means by which extraneous heat, as opposed to Innate Heat, enters our body.

Food may be light, heavy, or of medium quality. Light food produces thin blood. Heavier food produces thick blood. A medium in this regard is the food that produces a medium type of blood.

Food may also be rich or poor in quality. Examples are:

- Rich and light: wine, meat juice, partially fried or hard boiled eggs.
- Poor and heavy food, poor in nutrition that forms only a small quantity of thick blood: cheese, partially fried meat and eggplant.
- Poor and light: honey diluted with rose water, vegetables of a medium quality, apples and pomegranates.
- Rich and heavy: fried eggs and beef.

All of these may be further defined according to the nature of resulting chyme, as wholesome and unwholesome:

- Light, rich, and wholesome: egg yolks and raw meat juice.
- Light, rich, and unwholesome: chicken, and young pheasants.
- Light, poor, and wholesome: lettuce and apples.
- Light, poor, and unwholesome: radish, mustard and most vegetables.
- Heavy, rich, and wholesome: boiled eggs and meat of a young lamb.
- Heavy, rich, and unwholesome: beef and duck.
- Heavy, poor, and unwholesome: dried meat.
- Heavy, poor, and wholesome: lean beef.

CONCERNING FOOD THAT WE EAT

In seeking to maintain health, care must be taken that the essential basis of the meal is not just in nutrients like vegetables, fruits, and suchlike. The reason for this is because foods that are weak in temperament over oxidize our blood, while those that are dense render our blood phlegmatic and our body heavy.

OUR APPETITE

According to Avicenna, we should not eat unless we are hungry, nor should we delay our meal until our appetite has gone. This rule does not apply in the case of a false appetite met with intoxicated individuals or the subjects of nausea. If we are fasting and continue fasting, our stomach will fill up with decaying humours.

THE QUANTITY OF OUR FOOD

Nothing is worse, he says, than for us to overeat during a time of plenty after having been in a state of starvation during a time of famine, and vice versa. But the transition period is the worst. For we often see many people who lack food at a time of famine, and eat to repletion when a fertile year comes with fatal results. Great repletion is very dangerous in any case, whether in regard to food or to drink.

Indications that our meal is moderate include the following: our pulse does not become full; our breathing does not become shallow. The latter only occurs if our stomach is compressing the diaphragm, thus making breathing shallow and short. The pressure to be met by the heart increases after a large meal. As the force of our heart does not diminish, our pulse becomes large and full.

THE ORDER OF THE FOOD THAT WE EAT

Those of us who are desirous of maintaining our health need to be watchful of the order in which the components of a meal are taken. For example, we should not consume a tenuous food that is rapidly digested after consuming a very nutritious dish that is slowly digested such as eating a steak dinner followed by a bowl of fresh fruit. The reason for this is because the initial article of food will be digested first and therefore float over the other, unable to enter our blood. Consequently it ferments and decomposes, and in addition sets up decomposition of the food next taken. The reverse order, therefore, is the one we need to adopt, so that the easily digestible foods will pass on with the other into the intestine, and then undergo complete digestion.

Fish and similar articles of food should not be consumed after laborious work or exercise because they undergo decomposition and then decompose the humours.

An error in eating or drinking any nutrients is to be corrected according to the digestion and maturation. We must protect ourselves from the nature that is likely to arise. To affect this, we should consume the opposite substance until our digestion is completed. For example, if our nourishment is cold (i.e., Cucumber, Lettuce), temper it with its opposite (i.e., Onions, Leeks). If our nourishment is hot, temper it with the opposite (i.e., broccoli). If our nourishment is binding, eat food that will open and evacuate, and then fast for a suitable period. In this state—and this is true for all who wish to maintain their health—we should not consume food until there is a definite appetite, and unless the stomach and upper small intestine have emptied themselves of the previous meal, because there is nothing more harmful to our body than to super impose digestive matter upon incompletely digested food.

There is also nothing worse than causing nauseous indigestion, especially when this is the result of bad foods. If these are heavy, the following symptoms and imbalances arise: pain in the joints, in the kidneys; difficult or labored breathing, gout, hardening and enlargement of the spleen and liver, imbalances in which the phlegmatic or black bile humours are concerned. If our foods thin our blood, then acute fevers, severe fevers, and grave acute inflammatory disturbances would develop.

Aids to Our Digestion

It is sometimes very necessary to eat foods on the top of another food, by way of food. For example, if we eat sharp and salty nutrients, we can then eat moist-tempered nourishments that have no flavor before the former have digested completely. The chyme by which the body is nourished is then corrected. The contrary holds good if we eat heavier foods and afterwards consume a food that is quickly digested and acrid in taste. These are suitable measure for aiding our digestion.

Our Food and Exercise

A small amount of movement or activity after a meal allows the food to descend to our stomach, especially if after this there is a desire to sleep. Mental excitement, emotion or vigorous exercise interferes with digestion.

The Size of Our Meals

In regard to the quantity of food eaten during a meal, none of our meals should be bulky enough to completely satisfy our appetite. We should stop eating while some appetite or desire for food is still present, for such remnants of hunger will disappear in the course of an hour. A meal is injurious when it brings heaviness to our stomach, and Wine is injurious when it exceeds moderation, and swims in the stomach.

If we eat in excess one day, we should fast the next, and sleep longer in a place that is not too hot or too cold. If you cannot sleep, try a light walking exercise even around the house. It is nourishing to drink a glass of pure wine during this time. Try to avoid resting or lying down right away as well.

Our Food and Sleep

A short nap after a meal is useful, as long as it is not a bulky or heavy meal as mentioned above. Avicenna says we can help aid digestion during a nap or sleep by doing the following: (1) Lying down on our right side, then on the left, and finally turning back again to our right side in the span of a few minutes. (2) Covering our body with ample warmth from our blanket. (3) Making sure our neck is slightly raised.

The standard size of the meal depends on usage and vigor. A normally robust person should eat until satisfied so long as they do not feel a sense of heaviness. Avoid fast bodily movements while eating. This can cause subsequent rumbling in our stomach or splashing of the food. While eating, it's important that you feel good and not nauseous, have a canine appetite, loss of appetite, or sleeplessness. In addition, the taste of our food should not repeat if and when we burp. If the taste of food lingers in our mouth a very long time after the meal, it shows that the dish was too heavy.

Our Food and Nature

The following should be observed: those of us who experience a sense of heat and flushing after a meal should not consume a whole meal in one sitting, but instead, consume the meal in small portions in short intervals. This will help us to avoid the effects of repletion such as shivering followed by a sense of heat, similar to the feeling of a low-grade fever.

Those of us who cannot digest the amount of food appropriate for ourselves should increase the number of articles of diet, but diminish the quantity.

If we have an Airy (hot and wet) temperament, we primarily need to eat foods that are cold and dry. If we have a Fiery (hot and dry) temperament, we need a diet that consists of cold and wet foods. If we are a Watery (cold and wet) temperament generating phlegmatic blood, we need feebly nutritious articles of diet that are hot and dry. Those of us with an Earthy (cold and dry) temperament need a diet that produces more heat and moisture and the least amount of cold and dryness.

The Prescription of Our Diet

Some of us have a mode of behavior of our stomach whereby food leaves it very rapidly and does not stay in it long enough to undergo gastric digestion. This explains the necessity for taking the behavior of our stomach and its nature into consideration [along with other factors when drawing up a diet].

There are some of us in whom thinning food, instead of being digested quickly as it should, undergoes decomposition in our stomach, whereas less rapidly digestible foods are digested more readily. If we have this type of stomach, we are called Fiery-tempered. Others of us are exactly the opposite. Therefore the rules to be given must be adapted to the peculiarity of each of us.

The countries in which we live also have their own natural properties that are distinct from the ordinary rule. This must also be borne in mind. A test must be made to ascertain what the rule should be. Thus, a food that is often consumed, though injurious to a certain degree, may be more appropriate for a given individual than a food that we do not often consume, even though its character is good.

Then again, there is a food that is to be regarded as appropriate to everyone's physique and nature. To change from such a diet would prove injurious and detrimental to us. Good and laudable foods may be injurious to some. We should therefore avoid them. But those of us who are able to digest a bad food should not be deceived, because, for all we know, we will some day give rise to bad humours and the consequent obstinate ailments.

PALATABILITY

We should remember, too, that nourishment is best when it has the most agreeable flavor. This is because the walls of our stomach and our power of retention jointly apply themselves better to a food of good substance. Also, the efficiency of our retentive power is assisted when the principal members all mutually concur the nature of one being not more divergent from that of another than natural. Avicenna says that this is the requisite condition. The conditions are not fulfilled, for instance, if the natures are not normal, or alike in the respective members. Thus, the nature of the liver may differ to an unnatural extent from that of the stomach. Among unpleasant influences arising from enjoying the taste of poor nourishments is that we may be tempted to eat too freely of them even though we know it is not good for us.

THE RULES TO BE OBSERVED AFTER MEALS

EXERCISE

Refrain from vigorous exercise after a meal, in case the food passes into our blood before it is sufficiently digested, glides out of our stomach without being digested at all, or undergoes decomposition, since exercise disturbs our gastric nature.

HUNGER AND THIRST

To go to sleep while thirsty is beneficial to cold and moist temperaments, but is injurious to those of us whose temperament is too warm because of the yellow bile humour being too plentiful. The same is true in regards to going to sleep while fasting, or skipping a meal.

The yellow bile humour becomes dominant in individuals who skip meals, as the humour begins to flow into the stomach. Therefore, when we eat any food, it decomposes. The same symptoms occur within us when we are asleep or awake when food corrupts. This explains the loss of desire for food.

When there is loss of appetite for food, something needs to be consumed to counteract this feeling and relax our bowels. For this purpose something mild, like fruit, should be eaten, or a snack that does not cause you nausea. Normal meals may be resumed after our appetite has returned.

SWEETS

Sweet foods readily produce obstructions in the channels of our body because the attractive power draws them into our blood before they have been properly digested. Obstructions culminate in various imbalances such as edema or swelling caused by excess fluid's trapped in the body's tissues.

EXCESSIVE HEAT IN THE STOMACH

If we are among those whose alimentary tract is hot and strong and we eat heavy food, it will give rise to gas in the stomach and fermentative aliment. When we consume a blood-thinning article of food on an empty stomach, the latter contracts on it. If we then eat something heavy, our stomach abandons the blood-thinning food and ceases digesting it. As a consequence, it undergoes decay. This can be avoided by allowing an interval of time to elapse between the two kinds of food. Under these circumstances, it is best to eat the heavy food slowly because then the hold that the stomach has on the blood-thinning food is not broken.

CONCERNING WHAT WE DRINK

DRINKING WATER

Water is the only element that has the special property of entering into the composition of foods and drinks—not that it is itself a nutriment (although it will by itself prolong life for some time), but rather that it enables chyme to penetrate into our body and permeate and purify its substance.

Avicenna Cuisine does not wish to imply that water does not nourish at all, but we mean that it is not, as nutriment is, potential blood, giving rise ultimately to our body tissue. As an elementary substance, it is not changed in a state in such a way as to become able to receive the "form" of blood or of tissue. This can only occur with a true compound.

Water is really a "substance" that helps to make chyme fluid and attenuated so that it can flow easily into the blood vessels and out of the excretory channels. Nutrition cannot be effective without it. It is the handmaid of nutrition.

We should avoid drinking an excess amount of water after a meal because it causes the food to leave the coats of the stomach and float about. It's better to wait and not drink fluids until our food has left our stomach, which is made evident through the sensation of lightness in the upper part of our abdomen. However, if you have an urgent thirst, you should drink little sips of cold water, preferably through a straw. The colder the water, the less you will require. This amount of cold water will soothe your stomach and keep the food together.

Drinking Wine and the Stages of Being Inebriated

White Light Wine is best for those who are in a heated state, for it does not cause headaches. However, it does sometimes retain moisture. It may relieve a headache when it has to do with heat in the stomach.

Heavy Wine, if sweet, is best for those of us who want to put on weight and become strong, but we must beware of developing obstructions. Old Red Wine is best for those of us who have a Watery—phlegmatic temperament (cold and wet).

Avicenna says it is not good to drink Wine directly after any of the various meals throughout the day for the reason we have already explained. Wine should only be consumed once digestion occurs and food has passed into our small intestine. Drinking Wine directly after eating causes bad chyme to be absorbed and pass into the remote parts of the body. The same is true if Wine is consumed after eating Fruit, especially Melons.

Wine is beneficial for those of us who are predominately of a Fiery temperament (hot and dry) because it gets rid of the excess of this temperament by provoking the urine. It is good for those of us who have a Watery temperament because it matures moisture. The better its aroma and taste, the more beneficial.

Wine is also very efficient in causing the products of digestion to become dispersed through our body. It cuts phlegm and disperses it. It also separates the yellow bile humour (Fiery-tempered, hot and dry) and draws it into the urine. It renders the black bile humours (Earthy-tempered, cold and dry) more mobile and able to leave the system. Wine counteracts the harmful influence of this black bile humour by contrariety and breaks up all entanglements without the necessity of extraneous heat.

Wine does not readily inebriate a person with a vigorous brain because the brain is not susceptible to ascending harmful gaseous products nor does it take up heat from the Wine to any degree beyond what is useful. Therefore, the brain makes its mental power clearer than before. Other talents are not affected in such an advantageous manner. The effect is different on people who are not of this caliber.

A person who is weak in the chest, to the extent that breathing is difficult during the wintertime, should not wisely drink very much Wine.

If Wine has an injurious effect on the body and is heating to the liver, your diet should include some dishes containing, for instance, the juice of (sour) Unripe Grapes, and the like, and foods that are generally served with Wine after a meal (dessert), such as Pomegranate, and tart things like Citruses.

If the Wine is liable to go to the head, one should drink less and try to dilute and clarify the Wine. After the meal, it is then good to eat a fruit, like Quince for instance with your Wine.

As you know, old Wine is like a food. It is only slightly nutritious. New Wine clogs the liver and produces an inflamed liver by giving rise to copious gas. Avicenna says the best Wine to drink is that which is clear, white, tending to a red tinge, of good bouquet, neither tart nor sweet in taste, neither old nor new.

If you have a distressing feeling come about after drinking Wine, you should drink Pomegranate Juice, cold water and syrup of Absinthe next morning. After this, eat your breakfast and take a hot bath.

Wine that is thoroughly diluted softens the stomach, makes it humid and relieves thirst. Diluted Wine intoxicates quickly because the watery constituent takes it quickly into the blood.

Frequent intoxication breaks down the temperament of the liver and brain, weakens the nerves and tends to produce diseases of the nervous system, unconsciousness or incapacity resulting from a cerebral hemorrhage or stroke, and sudden death.

When excess Wine or alcohol is drunk, your body temperament changes. In some cases, it can turn into a bad kind of yellow bile humour (hot and dry) or, in other cases, into pure Vinegar. In both cases, the changes in the stomach are very injurious.

The most detrimental of the effects of Wine is that upon the brain. That is why those who are not strong in that way should drink the very least amount of Wine and diluted. Avicenna says to give Wine to youths is like adding fire to a fire already prepared with matchwood.

For those who do like to drink Wine frequently, it is advantageous to include Cabbage simmered with Meat for instance in their menu. Anything that lightens the fumes of the Wine is also helpful, for instance Cumin, Cardamom and more particularly, any nourishments which are viscous and glutinous, for they aggregate the fumes (i.e., oily, sweet and viscous articles of food) and prevent intoxication in spite of drinking so much Wine, by restraining the rapidity with which the Wine enters the blood.

Intoxication is rapid: (1) when there is weakness of the brain; (2) when there is an abundance of humours; (3) when the Wine is strong; (4) when the food is scanty; (5) when the regimen is itself depraved; and (6) when the Wine is taken continuously (for a long time).

According to Avicenna, the following syrup stops intoxication: One part juice of White Cabbage; one part juice of unripe Pomegranate, a half-part of Vinegar. Simmer these ingredients for a few minutes and drink one ounce before drinking Wine.

For those recovering from intoxication, Avicenna says to drink water and Vinegar several times, one after the other. It also helps to sniff at Camphor and Sandalwood. You can also place cold ingredients on your head such as Rose Oil and Wine Vinegar.

The following are the various effects of our mind being intoxicated, not arranged chronologically: First, our recognition of truth is impaired, and the operation of our mind is imperfect. The intellectual power falls in proportion. The substrate continues to attract our breath until our temperament reaches up to that of the alcohol after which the flow of our breath comes to an end.

The power of our mind has a greater affinity for joy during the state of intoxication. The pleasing feelings that come to our mind do not reach it by the usual route between the senses and the imagination because the senses dominate perception. Our breath becomes full with moisture, which alters its strength. At this point, our senses dominate our inner breath and are more powerful than our understanding.

Things being so, it makes sense that a person's conception of the future, of beauty, of rational affairs, has become blurred in an intoxicated person's mind. Our perception of sweet and delectable foods prevails. The sense of the present is very strong. It is the very strength of this tendency that accounts for the fact that quite a slight situation will evoke happiness and amusement. While inebriated, we also notice things less particularly the more often we encounter them.

PART III

Dietetics

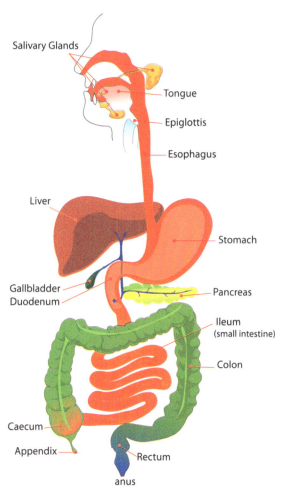

CHAPTER 14

On Digestion and Related Matters

WITH AVICENNA CUISINE IT IS VITAL TO understand the interrelationships between the four elements of air, fire, water and earth, the four qualities of the elements, namely, hot, cold, wet and dry, the four humours of blood, yellow bile, phlegm and black bile and the four temperaments of Airy, Fiery, Watery and Earthy.

As has been pointed out, the four elements are not elements of what we know as the periodic table of elements even though the word "element" has traditionally been used in the English translation of the word from Greek, Syriac, Persian, Arabic, Urdu or other languages. The four "elements" of air, fire, water and earth are part of everything created and part of our own local weather report.

With Avicenna Cuisine, it is the qualities of these classical elements that are most relevant. Air is actively hot and passively wet. Fire is actively hot and passively dry. Water is actively cold and passively wet. Earth is actively cold and passively dry. According to Avicenna, while everything other than the human being is formed from these elemental qualities, within the human being these elemental qualities form the humours at the time of conception from the "sperms" of our parents as the humours are four fluids that are all contained within the first clot of blood.

THE FOUR STAGES OF DIGESTION

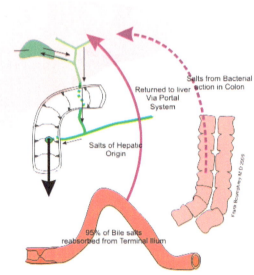

Enterohepatic circulation of Bile salts

Recycling of the Bile

According to Avicenna, digestion takes place through four stages driven by the energy of the Natural Drive, the major organ of which is the liver. The energy for this Natural Drive comes from both our Innate Heat (or thermal energy) and our "Breath of Life" (kinetic energy). The action of these two sources of energy in the liver, as previously discussed, develop the four humours from the chyme produced by the digestive process. The four Assistants to the digestive process are: Attraction, Retention, Digestion and Elimination. The blood humour includes the Attraction Assistant to digestion. This gives it the ability to attract its nourishment to itself. The yellow bile (bilious) humour includes the Digestion Assistant. This allows it to digest the food that we eat. The black bile humour (atrabile) operates the Retentive Assistant. This assistant dries, condenses and solidifies chyme. Finally, the phlegmatic humour (serous) contains the Elimination Assistant to digestion. This allows the chyme to be expelled and wash out any putrefaction. These four humours are the main suppliers of our nutrition and metabolism.

Digestion begins from the time of mastication as the lining of our mucous membrane of our mouth is in direct contact with the mucosa of our stomach. Our food is altered by its contact with the lining of our mouth. Saliva aids our digestion further by its own activity.

Our stomach digests food, not only through thermal energy provided by Innate Heat, but also by the heat of our surrounding organs such as our spleen on the left. It is true that our spleen is cold-tempered, but due to its rich fluid-carrying vessels, it also provides heat to our stomach. There is, also, in front, the omentum (a fold of peritoneum extending from our stomach to adjacent abdominal organs) whose fat easily retains heat and reflects it onto our stomach. Above is our heart that warms our diaphragm and so warms our stomach.

The First Stage or Attraction

The first stage of our digestion gives the essence of the digested material that becomes chyme (a milky bodily fluid consisting of lymph and emulsified fats, or free fatty acids) with the help of mixing with the fluid it has consumed. The chyme is of the consistency of a broth, as thick as sodden barley. The part of this chyme that is thus diluted is drawn from our stomach into our intestines and eventually reaches our liver.

THE SECOND STAGE OR DIGESTION

This chyme is then sent to our liver by our Innate Heat or thermal energy to produce the four humours. By being distributed over the whole liver, the chyme is exposed to the digestive function of our whole organ. The function of the liver to produce the four humours is thus accomplished most vigorously, energetically, and speedily.

THE THIRD STAGE OR RETENTION

The change of nutriment into the blood humour is now complete. The blood and its other humours, while in circulation, undergo a third digestion when the chyme actually reaches the tissues. The chyme then travels along finer divisions until it comes to our capillaries (the very fine hair-like channels), which are the ultimate source of our vein, carrying our blood to our heart. These channels are, however, so narrow that food can only pass through them with the help of serous humour.

THE FOURTH STAGE OR EVACUATION

This is the stage of the removal of waste materials from our body.

THE BY-PRODUCTS OF DIGESTION

The various products and by-products of digestion up to this point are the result of a digestion producing a healthy blood humour. By-products of this digestive process include a foam that is the bilious humour and a sort of accelerant that is the black bile humour.

Yellow bile humour in our stomach produces stomach acid and yellow bile. This is where most of the breakdown of nourishment occurs where a black bile humour dries the superfluous matter from the liver.

In unhealthy digestion, by-products include: (1) an oxidation product where digestion is carried too far—a thinned portion shows a diseased yellow bile humour, and a dense portion shows a diseased black bile humour; and (2) a product when digestion is not carried far enough, which is the phlegmatic humour.

As long as the blood humour that our liver forms stays in our liver and is thinner than it should be because of the presence of the phlegmatic humour, it is healthy. When the blood humour leaves our liver, the excess phlegmatic humour is removed. It is taken to the renal vessels and so provides the kidneys with the quantity and quality of our blood humour best suited for their nutrition. The fat of our blood humour nourishes our kidneys and the superfluous wateriness. A certain degree of blood humour passes down to our bladder and so away from our body while our good blood humour ascends into our veins and enters into the main channel from where it spreads into the smaller branches until it reaches the tissues.

THE CAUSES OF THE FORMATION OF THE HUMOURS

What is it that causes the humours to develop? The material cause is the change or movement determined by the changes being made. The formal cause is the account of what the humour is to be. The efficient cause plays a role in changing the humours within us, based on the elemental qualities of what we eat being hot, cold, wet or dry in addition to the Six

Nurturing Essentials. The final cause is the completion and perfection of the humours.

The **material causes** of the formation of blood humour are those parts of the solid and fluid digestive material which produce an equable temperament; of the yellow bile humour are the thinned hot, sweet, oily and sharp by-product of digested material; of the phlegmatic humour are the dense, humid, thick, cold by-product of the digested material; of the black bile humour are the very dense by-product of the digested material, very deficient in moisture and exceeding in heat.

The **formal causes** of the formation of blood humour are good digestion; of yellow bile humour are a digestion verging on excess; of the phlegmatic humour, imperfect digestion; and of the black bile humour, a tendency occurring with undue rapidity preventing flow or dispersal.

The **efficient causes** of the formation of the blood humour are modified heat; of yellow bile humour, modified heat for normal yellow bile humour (foam), and undue heat for abnormal yellow bile humour whose site is the liver; for phlegmatic humour, feeble heat; for black bile humour are medium heat (that is, a heat of oxidation which surpasses the limits of equipoise).

Further details regarding the efficient causes include the following: We must not forget that the most fundamental agents in the formation of our humours are heat and cold. When heat is equable, blood humour forms. When heat is in excess, yellow bile humour forms. When in great excess so that oxidation occurs, black bile humour forms. When the cold is equable, phlegmatic humour forms. When cold is in excess so that solidification becomes dominant, black bile humour forms. When our black bile humour is plentiful, it virtually lodges between our liver and stomach with the result that our formation of blood humour and healthy fluids is interfered with and less blood humour is formed.

As to the **final cause** for the formation of blood humour, it is to nourish the body. For the yellow bile humour, the primary cause is nutrition or thinning while the secondary cause is cleansing the bowel wall and urge to evacuate. For the phlegmatic humour, the primary purpose is to thin the blood humour and the secondary purpose is to help it move through the narrow meridians or channels. For the black bile humour, the primary and secondary purposes include nutrition, the thickening or condensing of the blood humour, nourishment of the spleen, tone to the stomach, and aid to the appetite.

The Waste Products of the Digestive Process

There are four main ways for the digestive process to eliminate its wastes that build up within us. In the same way that with each breath we inhale, we exhale its waste, so with the foods that we consume.

The waste products of the first digestion in the stomach are eliminated through the intestines. Those of the second digestion in the liver are mostly eliminated through urine and it is only a small portion that is directed towards the gallbladder and spleen. Wastes from the third and fourth digestion are eliminated partly through sweat, ear, nasal and aural secretions and partly through the invisible pores of the body as well as through feces. If we are among those with thin humours, we are apt to be easily debilitated by wastes. This is particularly true if our bodily pores naturally produce a greater dispersion and thus cause loss of vitality.

As long as the chyme stays in the liver, the blood humour that the liver forms is thinner than it should be because of phlegmatic humour being in excess. When the blood humour leaves our liver, the excess phlegmatic humour is removed and taken to the renal vessels where it provides the kidneys with the quantity and quality of the blood humour best suited for their nutrition. The "fat" of the blood humour nourishes our kidneys and the superfluous phlegmatic humour and a certain degree of blood humour passes down to the bladder and so away from the body.

Lastly, it must be clearly understood that not only the causes of origin, but also the causes of movement of the humours must be taken into consideration. Exercise and heating agents set the blood, yellow bile, and even the black bile humour (which is thereby strengthened) in motion. Rest sets the phlegmatic humour in motion and strengthens it. Rest also strengthens some kinds of black bile humour. Even imagination, emotional states and other agents cause the humours to move.

Excessive Humours

Excessive humoural changes may be quantitative or qualitative: quantitative in regard to the meridians and qualitative in regard to energy levels. In quantitative excessive humours, the humours and Vital Energy are of a balanced quality, but so excessive in quantity that our vessels become swollen. In these cases, exertion is apt to cause a rupture of our blood vessels with the humours blocking the meridians or "passages." Avicenna Cuisine says this type of excessive humour can be treated by donating blood.

In the case of qualitative excessive humour, the problem is not in terms of the quantity of humours, but in unhealthiness of quality whereby the energy-givers are ineffective in the processes of digestion and maturation. A person who is in this state is in danger of putrefactive or infectious disorders.

Speaking in general of the signs of quantitative excessive humours, they are either objective or subjective. Objective results in sluggish movements or gestures while subjective signs are dreams in which there is a sense of weight—as when one dreams one is unable to move or is carrying a heavy weight or cannot give utterance to words. This kind of dream may be compared with that associated with the weakening of the humours. When the humours are moderate in amount, we may dream that we are flying through the air or moving at a great speed.

THE DOMINANCE OF BLOOD HUMOUR (AIR, HOT AND WET)

The signs of the dominance of the blood humour resemble those of quantitative excess and are characterized by our feelings of heaviness in our body, especially behind our eyes, over our head and across our temples. Stretching and yawning is frequent with this individual. There is a tendency to excessively sleep and our mind becomes dull. Occasionally, the excess of blood humour can be recognized from our temperament, age, residence and previous habits. Our characteristic dreams are of seeing excessive red things i.e., the sight of a large quantity of blood being lost or someone being soaked in blood or some other such vision.

THE DOMINANCE OF THE YELLOW BILE HUMOUR (FIRE, HOT AND DRY)

The signs of the dominance of yellow bile humours are yellow coloration in our eyes and complexion, bitter taste in our mouth, rough and dry tongue and dryness of our nostrils. Cool breezes are generally comforting to this individual. Additional signs are excessive thirst, rapidity of pulse and lack of appetite. Temperament, age, occupation, residence, climate and previous habits also help in determining this bodily state. Our characteristic dreams are of flames of fire and waves of yellow color.

The Dominance of the Phlegmatic Humour (Water, Cold and Wet)

The signs of the dominance of phlegmatic humour are excessive pallor, flabbiness of the body, cold and moist skin, excessive salivation and thick saliva. There is a reduced feeling of thirst, especially in the elderly, and particularly so when the phlegm is sour. A weak digestion may include excessive sleepiness and flabbiness of our muscles. Age, occupation, residence and previous history are also helpful in identifying the predominance of phlegmatic humour. We may dream of water, canals, cold, ice, rain and thundering hailstorms.

The Dominance of the Black Bile Humour (Earth, Cold and Dry)

The characteristic signs of the dominance of black bile humour are thick and dark blood, presence of anxiety and a false appetite. Age, temperament, habits, residence and occupation are also helpful in determining this. Our dreams are usually full of anxiety and often of dark places, dark trenches and dark fearful objects

On the Defects in Digestion

Having digestion problems? One of the following could be the cause:

- The lower parts of our stomach are damaged.
- The amount and type of food we consume;
- Our condition and rest;
- An imbalanced humour;
- A cold imbalanced humour, which does the most harm to our stomach;
- A dry imbalance, which can lead to depression; and
- A wet imbalanced humour that can cause edema.

ON REST AND ACTIVITY

Good digestion in our stomach requires adequate rest and sleep. If movement and lack of sleep take the place of rest and sleep, digestion does not properly occur. In other words, if the food that has entered our stomach is heavy and thick, digestion takes time, is incomplete, or does not occur at all. On the other hand, if light food is not digested, it will not stay in our stomach very long. If our stomach is unable to digest this light food, it will quickly putrefy.

Innate Heat is that which protects the humors from being overruled by foreign calorific agents. If our Innate Heat is strong, the Natural Drive and its Assistants are able to work through the humours and maintain digestion and maturation providing a healthy state. Extraneous or foreign "heat" cannot interfere with this so the humours do not undergo putrefactive decomposition. If the foreign calorific agent is feeble, the Natural Drive and its Assistants are unable to regulate the humors because the intermediary between the Natural Drive and its Assistants and the humors is enfeebled. Stagnation sets in and foreign heat now finds the humors no longer opposed to its action. It overcomes them. It utilizes them in its own way, and imparts a foreign movement to them. The result is what is known as "putrefaction."

Therefore, it is clear that Innate Heat is the instrument of all the drives, whereas coldness can only help them secondarily. That is why we speak of "Innate Heat," but not of "innate cold;" and why that which is proportionate to heat is not comparable with cold.

ON IMPERFECT DIGESTION

When food enters our stomach, it may be completely digested or partially digested. If it is partially digested, it does not convert to the humoural matter needed by our body. When our body does not receive enough nutrition from this partially digested food, we lose weight. Another reason for lack of nutrition may be because food is not being digested in our stomach at all. More clearly, the food either enters our stomach, but does not change at all, or the food changes, but it does so badly and putrefies.

When digestion does not occur, putrefaction of the food can be at any stage of digestion: first, second, third or fourth. This state of our stomach can result in many illnesses because the blood humour produced is not compatible with our temperament. As a result, the organs do not accept it, in which case the food putrefies.

The other digestive possibility is that the organs accept the food, but the immature blood humour does not turn into the nourishment that the organs need. If this occurs, the incompletely digested food that does not produce good blood humour has too much sediment or heat, which causes the stool to become black. If there is imbalanced black bile humour in the stomach, our stool becomes tar-colored.

If no digestion occurs at all, and the food is still intact and without any changes, we can develop intestinal slipping and sliding. This indigestion can cause tympanic edema when our stomach does not digest some part of the food and converts it to steam.

If a humour is the cause of stomach disability, its treatment during the digestive process is much easier than the treatment of an extreme imbalance. When food is not digested in our stomach, there is a reason for this. We need to find the reason for this and consume foods that are the opposite temperament to treat and brings our self back to balance.

ON THE CAUSES OF UNDIGESTED FOOD PUTREFYING

- The food is a type that increases our appetite so we continue to eat even though we are not hungry.
- Our stomach is full but we continue to eat anyway.
- Food enters our stomach too quickly and the previous food consumed is not digested by the time the new food reaches our stomach.
- Our first meal of the day has digested and left our stomach, but we fail to do any mild exercise before our second meal.
- The order in which we consumed our food is not healthy, i.e. first eating a food that takes a long time to digest and after that eating a light and quickly digestible food. The quickly digested food then sits on top of the slow to digest food, floating in our stomach and putrefying.
- We ate food and shortly after we moved in some way so as to cause the food in our stomach to move, which caused it to putrefy.
- We drank too many liquids after eating.
- We did not consume any liquids at all after eating.
- We are full from eating and have sexual intercourse immediately after that.
- Eating different types of food that confuse the digestive system.
- We swim or bathe after eating.

- We are exposed very cold or hot weather.
- We already have excess gas already in our stomach.

ON INDIGESTION AND ITS RESULTS

Indigestion can be very harmful. Indigestion is the mother of diseases and the source of bodily problems.

ON THE CAUSES OF INDIGESTION

- Yellow bile humour in our stomach does not cause indigestion, but it causes food to putrefy in our stomach.
- Unusual black bile humour in our stomach can cause both indigestion and the putrefaction of food inside our stomach.
- The stomach's dry or wet imbalance can be involved in digestion. They never completely destroy digestion, they just weaken it.
- The food inside our stomach might be evacuated from our stomach before it has been well digested.

ON THE TREATMENT OF INDIGESTION

If the cause of indigestion is minimal or it is from the accumulation of food in our stomach for a long period of time, the following can be helpful:

- Sleep a great deal and stop exercising.
- Avoid taking baths.
- Eat a small amount of light, thin and gentle foods.
- Massage hands and feet with olive and floral oils.
- Pour lukewarm water on our hands and feet.
- Avoid eating anything during the daytime.
- May help to consume a laxative healer, like prunes
- Black pepper is one of the best remedies to help cure digestion.
- Sleep as much as possible, especially on our right side. When we sleep on our left side, our liver covers our stomach. Sleeping on our right side helps food move down from our stomach due to the fact that in this position our stomach is straight.

If our stomach's hot imbalance with humoural matter is the cause for the disability of our stomach indigestion, a great remedy is oxymel (honey and vinegar) with Fresh Quince. You should also eat foods with an astringent effect and a sour taste, such as light and thin slices of Cooked Meat flavored with a sour and acrid taste which are considered cold-tempered foods and spices.

On Stomach Gas (Flatulence) and the Various Types

If wet-tempered food accumulates in our stomach and moisture enters our stomach from the temperament of the food, this can convert to gas. If our stomach's hot humoural imbalance is not extreme (even if it is moderate) it cannot prevent the food from converting to gas.

If the accumulated food in our stomach is disabled and no longer able to convert to gas by itself, and the stomach's hot imbalance is weak and insufficient for this purpose, the food can still change to gas. This type of food does not make or stimulate gas in our stomach, but if our stomach is weak and cannot digest it, it moves and gets mixed and remains undigested. This movement and mixing can stimulate gas. But if the heat in our stomach does not affect it at all, even a food with the ability to convert to gas will not convert to gas. In general, if a food does not create gas in our stomach, it is in one of the categories below:

- Heat in our stomach can be enough to digest the food completely without creating any gas, but we can do something to disturb the function of our stomach, such as drinking too much water after food or too much exercise after food, which causes the food in our stomach to move and produce gas.
- The food that has entered our stomach might have the ability to convert to gas, such as Beans, Lentils and others. When only a small amount of these foods enter our stomach and the heat of our stomach is not sufficiently hot, they will convert to gas.
- Thick, rich and sweet-tasting wine has the ability to convert to gas in our stomach unless the Sweet Wine is watery, but the gas that is created is gentle and silent.
- It may be that our stomach is empty, and clear when wet humoural matter enters our stomach and intestines. When our stomach's heat begins to work, it will digest this clear humoural matter, convert it to gas and create stomach-rumbling and gas.

- Black bile humour is collected in our stomach in a large amount and produces gas.
- A cold-tempered humoural matter comes from outside our stomach and accumulates in our body. Our digestive heat is weak or it does not have the ability to digest the whole humoural matter. It can only digest half of the humoural matter and the rest of the undigested half is vaporized and can convert to gas.

If the food we consume has the ability to convert to gas, we need to determine which type of food it is. If the food is good for our temperament, stomach gas will be weak and minimal. If we belch two or three times, this reduces the windiness in the gas and takes it away. If the cause of stomach gas is the humour inside our stomach, try drinking hot water.

In summary, we can find the sign for the source of stomach gas from food digestion. When we determine its cause, we need to treat the source. We need to avoid the causes and change our food and diet.

The difference between gas made from dry-tempered humour and gas from a wet-tempered humour is that the first one creates dry gas and the second one creates wet gas.

They said in the past that releasing gas from the back with noise and feces with less smell are signs of a strong stomach with good digestion. But this is not always the case. The truth is that releasing gas from the back without noise indicates a disabled stomach. However, this disability and difficulty in our stomach is less than the one that results in belching.

Gas with noise has two forms: if the gas noise is from the feces, the cause is pungency and grossness of feces. If the noisy gas is not from the feces and comes from the eliminative power, it is a sign of a strong stomach.

Gas released from the back without noise is a greater sign of a strong eliminative force by the stomach than noisy gas is (especially noisy gas that is released involuntarily). Noisy gas coming out involuntarily from the back is a sign of stomach anxiety.

If the smell from the feces is not too bad, that is a very good sign of well-digested food. On the other hand, strong, bad-smelling feces indicates a spoiled and damaged stomach. If the feces do not smell at all, it means that food has been hidden and remains in the stomach.

On Stomach Anxiety and Its Treatment

Sometimes we develop a type of depression that upsets us and our stomach. This depression can be due to a stomach imbalance that may cause sudden jumping, excitement and an abnormal heartbeat. This condition can also cause some obstructions and change our skin color. This color change is a warning for an upset stomach that can change into an anxious stomach.

The cause for this depressed stomach is the humoural matter, especially if that particular humoural matter was located inside our stomach and then drained. Our body cannot naturally treat the humoural matter by itself or move it away. Avicenna suggests drinking Quince Syrup, Sour Grape Syrup or fruit syrups alike as a remedy.

If stomach anxiety is mild, it is enough to just drink a mixture of ½ Wine, ½ water with a tonic healer to cleanse it. If it is severe, we need to use the treatment for an upset stomach.

If the stomach is depressed because of a hot-tempered humour in our stomach (this is usually the cause), cold and moist-tempered foods and herbs are the best treatment.

It may or may not be difficult for you to source these ingredients, but Avicenna suggests that if stomach depression is severe and greater than expected, rub a Sandalwood Poultice with Damask Rose and similar herbs on the stomach.

On the Diet for a Sensitive Stomach

Those who have a sensitive stomach need to have a diet that consists of foods that thicken our blood humour such as Red Meat and Whole Grains. Those with a sensitive stomach should also avoid delaying meals throughout the day. As soon you feel hungry, it's important to eat at least a snack right away.

CHAPTER 15

On the Signs of the States of Our Stomach

ON STOMACH PAIN

WHEN OUR STOMACH HURTS, THERE is a reason for it. It could be one of the following:

- We are eating a food with no nourishment, especially if it is hot and dry tempered.
- We may feel pain while we are eating. This indicates that our stomach is dominated by black bile humour.
- We may feel pain as soon as the food fills our stomach. This is sign of having yellow bile humour in our stomach that came from our liver and drained into our stomach.
- We may feel pain only after the food has been sitting in our stomach. This is because both stomach humours (black bile humour from the spleen and yellow bile humour from the liver) remain at the bottom of our stomach. There is no sensitivity there. As soon as food enters our stomach, the humour is stimulated by mixing with the food. This is when it comes up and reaches our stomach orifice, sticks there and disturbs it. Our stomach is the most sensitive internal organ and this is what causes the pain.
- We may eat when we are not even hungry. We keep eating and filling up our stomach. Our stomach gets tired from receiving so much food, digesting and storing it. This can cause stomach pain, burning and weakening.
- We may have stomach gas.
- We may be drinking extremely cold water

On Stomach Weakness

Inability of our stomach to digest food we have eaten may be for one of the following reasons:

- Our stomach does not have the power to digest nourishment.
- Our appetite sometimes is less than normal.
- With a weak stomach, we may want to eat food, but when we eat it, we will dislike it and do not eat it at all, or we eat a little and leave the rest.
- Stomach weakness can be the cause of all other diseases of the body.

On Appetite

On Abnormal Appetite

There are three groups of us with abnormal appetites. Some of us have too much appetite, some have no appetite and some have appetite but less then normal.

- If we are among those who have a cold and wet imbalanced temperament, we will crave cold drinks and have little appetite for food or less appetite for it.
- If we are among those that have a hot and dry imbalanced temperament, our condition will be the opposite. We will crave food more than we crave cold drinks.
- If our imbalance becomes very extreme, our appetite will completely disappear.
- Cold weather and the environment stimulate our appetite. That is why appetite increases in the winter.
- If the cause of loss of appetite is a moist, sticky and thick matter in our stomach, Avicenna says it is helpful to eat olives, a little salted fish and slowly sip wild garlic vinegar.

On Foods That Can Induce Appetite

The following can induce and be helpful for a person with a lack of appetite:

- Regular table salt
- Capers

- Mint
- Onion
- Olives
- Pepper
- Cloves
- Vinegar
- Pickled Vegetables

The following Mint Medicinal Syrup can induce appetite and also prevent nausea in those of us whose stomachs cannot accept food:

Prescription: Grind and squeeze a whole Pomegranate with its skin in a blender. Add ½ part Fresh Mint, ½ part water and ½ part Honey. Mix together in a pot and bring to a slow boil until it becomes a syrup. Drink a ½ teaspoon for breakfast on an empty stomach.

Most oils can destroy or reduce one's appetite because oil loosens the stomach and obstructs the orifice of the vessels. Only unripe Olive Oil and Pistachio Oil are healthier and do less harm to the stomach.

On Excessive Appetite

When we have an excessive appetite, we may not have an appetite, but other organs are hungry and crave food and nutrition. This is when we begin to eat excessively without appetite. In this situation, our vessels are empty of nutrition because they are not being nourished by our stomach. Sometimes this hunger becomes so severe that it causes us to faint. This type is usually seen those of us who travel in cold weather and are stricken with cold. Eating junk food often can cause excessive appetite because our body is constantly searching for nourishment that it never receives.

On Excessive Thirst

Extreme thirst and becoming thirsty more than normal is a sign of a disability in our body. What is the reason for this and what causes it?

- Extreme heat in our body caused by hot and dry foods and drinks;
- Our stomach's hot imbalanced temperament;
- Constantly eating and drinking very salty foods and drinks; and
- Our stomach may fill with bitter tasting yellow bile humour.

- Other organs may be involved in causing extreme thirst such as happens with diabetes.
- Talking more than normal can cause thirst.
- Too much exercise can lead to excessive thirst.
- Getting too tired can make us thirsty.
- Sleeping after eating hot-tempered foods may make us thirsty.

On Determining the States of Our Stomach

In order to determine the state and sensations of our stomach, we can use the following signs:

Food

1   Does our stomach have the ability to keep food down or not?
2   Can it digest food easily or not?
3   Does it send digested food out or not?
4   Do we have a good appetite?
5   How is our appetite for drinks?
6   Are there any contractions and movement in our stomach?
7   Do we have hiccups? How often?
8   What kind of taste does our mouth and tongue have?
9   What taste do we like more and hate more?
10   How dry, moist, rough or smooth is our tongue?
11   How is the smell of our mouth?
12   Does gas from our body make noise or not?
13   Any gas coming up through our mouth through burping needs to be checked as well.
14   The inside of our mouth, its color and smell, is a guide as well.
15   Any pain and disturbances in our stomach.

Stool

If our stool is straight and even and has a medium color and smell and does not have a strong smell that means that our stomach has digested food properly. It is a sign of a strong balance. If food is not well digested, this is a sign of a stomach disabled by an imbalance. The color of the stool is a sign of the food in the stomach. Its softness, pungency and smell tells us what is in our stomach. If our stool is very soft with a bad smell, this means the food left our stomach before being digested. It did not stay there for a long enough time. This is due to the retentive force of our stomach. If the smell is very bad and it is not soft, this means that our digestive force is not working well in our stomach.

HICCUPS

If we feel caustic pain while hiccupping, it means that a fermented, strong in taste or bitter-tasting humour is in our stomach. If we sense our stomach stretching, it means gas has collected in our stomach. If we do not have these signs and do not feel thirsty, it is a sign of phlegmatic humour. If we get hiccups after cleansing our stomach or after a fever, it is a sign of having a dry temperament.

ON DIGESTION

How can we know if our stomach has properly digested food and there is no difficulty?

- If quickly after the food enters our stomach there is no heavy feeling or disturbance in our stomach.
- We have no stomach rumbling;
- No feeling of a bloated stomach;
- No belching; and
- No taste of smoke or sour flavor.
- There is no hiccupping.
- If our stomach does not pulsate and stretch after eating.
- If food does not stay in our stomach for a longer than normal time and it leaves our stomach on time.
- If we have a good sleep and do not wake up early.
- If our eyes do not swell after eating.

EMOTIONAL STRESS

Emotional stress and reaction can damage our stomach—it is very sensitive—and can cause seizures with muscle contractions. If we are among these people with very sensitive stomachs, any small cause or stress, such as anger, fasting, or depression, and any stimulant of a humour can damage our stomach.

If emotional stress causes caustic bitter humour to reach our stomach orifice because of the stomach's high sensitivity, we can have seizures that cause fainting and muscular contractions. This is because our brain can be involved in damaging our stomach orifice.

WEAK STOMACH

If we have a sensitive and weak stomach orifice, we have the same feeling as when our stomach orifice is injured. This means that if we are among those with a weak stomach orifice and we eat a great amount, drink too much alcohol or have sexual intercourse more than normal, we can develop seizures with muscular contractions. We may also develop yellow bile depression and have nightmares and insomnia.

It is important to know that if stomach disease becomes chronic and remains for a long time, this will loosen and weaken our stomach surface membrane. Treatment will be difficult.

Part IV

The Temperaments

CHAPTER 16

What is Temperament?

KNOWING OUR TEMPERAMENT IS VERY IMPORTANT and knowing that of our friends has great advantages. It helps us understand our "self" and others better. Without knowing something about our own temperament and that of others, it will be to our disadvantage to ill-treat our "self" and others. If we know our own defects and that of people we relate to, we will not be quick to anger in certain situations. We will be able to reflect back and realize that what we are witnessing is a problem of a different tempera-ment then that of our own. However, this can only happen when we are fully aware of our own temperament. This way we are able to judge our "self," our moods and past experiences. It also enables us to work towards completing and perfecting our "self" by recognizing both the strengths and weaknesses of our temperament. It will allow us to develop our temperament so that we feel good about our self.

Each one of us have an innate or "nature-born," predisposed temperament with which we were born, which is unique to each of us. As has been mentioned, this innate temperament is then either enhanced or changed by our nurturing process and the environment in which we grow up. It is important to note that whatever our innate temperament is, it is just as good as any other person's innate disposition even if it is very different.

Our temperament[2] is our soul that is activated by our mind in our thoughts, reflections, imaginings and memory based on the external stimuli we have received. Knowing our temperament answers questions we may have about our thinking, emotional and behavioral reaction to situations. How do we relate to others? How do we react when we deeply feel something? What is our response when someone praises us or when we are offended by something someone says or when we dislike someone? Do we respond quickly having become excited or slowly and calmly? Do we feel we have to act immediately or are we able to wait to respond? How long does the impression last in our mind? Are we able to quickly overcome our excitement or that we do not dwell on what has happened? If we are not aware of our natural, innate pre-disposition we will not be able to determine our reactions. They will just be our automatic pilot responding rather than our reflective response.

The word temperament is often used in a purely psychological sense, but in the sense of foods the major emphasis is on our physical body and our digestive system. This implies the state of our humours or our biological constitution. Our temperament is created by the mixing of our humours. The humours within the human body are similar to the four elements and their elemental qualities of hot, cold, wet and dry. Therefore, if we are determined to have an Airy temperament, this means that the dominant humour in our body is blood humour (hot and wet). If we have a Fiery temperament, this means that the dominant humour within us is the yellow bile humour (also known as bilious, hot and dry humour). In the same way having a Watery or cold and wet temperament means we have a dominance of phlegmatic humour (cold and wet), whereas an Earthy temperament means the dominance of black bile (cold and dry).

Once we know our primary temperament (we may also have a secondary temperament as we will see), and are careful in regard to the six nurturing essentials, we can maintain a balanced, individual temperament that will insure our good health. This balanced temperament occurs when we avoid too much of even something that is good. Or, we could be in a situation where we get too much heat, for instance, sunbathing on a beach or too much cold trying to conquer Mt. Everest or too much dryness or moisture. These latter two may be the result of a bad diet or stress or anxiety or depression or lack of exercise. All of these can create an imbalance in our temperament.

Socrates, one of the most renowned of the Greek sages, used and taught as an important axiom to Avicenna Cuisine: "Know yourself"—and an important part of it is learning what our temperament is.

THE FOUR PRIMARY TEMPERAMENTS

If we consider the reaction of various persons to the same experience, we will find that it is different in every one of them. It may be quick and lasting or slow but lasting. Or it may be quick but of short duration or slow and of short duration. Our manner of reaction, or the different degrees of excitability, is what we call "temperament." There are four primary temperaments: Airy, Fiery, Earthy, and Watery.

Our temperament, then, is a fundamental disposition of our soul, that manifests itself whenever an impression is made upon our mind, be that impression caused by thought—by thinking about something or by representation through the imagination—or by external stimuli. Knowledge of the temperament of any of us supplies the answer to the questions: How do I conduct myself? How do I feel moved to action whenever something impresses me strongly? For instance, how do I react, when I am praised or rebuked, when I am offended, when I feel sympathy for or aversion against somebody? Or, to use another example, how do I act if I am in a storm, or in a dark forest, or on a dark night when the thought of imminent danger comes to me?

On such occasions we may ask the following questions:

1   Are we under the influence of such impressions, thoughts or facts, quickly and vehemently excited or only slowly and superficially?

2   Do we undergo such influences or feel inclined to act quickly in order to oppose the impression or do we feel more inclined to remain calm and to wait?

3   Does our excitement last for a long time or only for a moment? Does the impression continue, so that at the recollection of such impression the excitement is renewed? Or do we conquer such excitement speedily and easily, so that the remembrance of it does not produce a new excitement?

The replies to these questions direct us to the four temperaments and furnish the key for the understanding of the temperament of each of us as individuals.

As Airy-tempered persons, we are quickly and strongly excited by the slightest impression and tend to react immediately, but the impression does not last. It soon fades away.

As Fiery-tempered persons, like the Airy, we are quickly and vehemently excited by any impression made. We tend to react immediately. The impression lasts a long time and easily induces new excitement.

As Watery-tempered persons, we are only slightly excited by any impression made upon us. We have scarcely any inclination to react, and the impression vanishes quickly.

As Earthy-tempered persons, at first we are only slightly excited by any impression received. A reaction does not set in at all or only after some time. But the impression remains deeply rooted, especially if new impressions of the same kind are repeated.

Fiery and Airy temperaments are extroverts and active. Earthy and Watery temperaments are introverts and passive. Fiery and Airy show a strong tendency to action. Earthy and Watery, on the contrary, are inclined to slow movement. Fiery and Earthy temperaments are of a passionate nature. They shake the very soul and act like an earthquake. The Airy and Watery are passionless temperaments. They do not lead to great and lasting mental excitement.

The Knowledge of Temperaments is Very Important

It may be difficult in many cases to decide upon our temperament. Still we should not permit ourselves to be discouraged in the attempt to understand our own temperament and that of those persons with whom we live or with whom we come often into contact, for the advantages of such insight are very great. To know the temperaments of our family and friends helps us to understand them better, treat them more correctly, and bear with them more patiently. These are evidently advantages for social life that can hardly be appreciated enough.

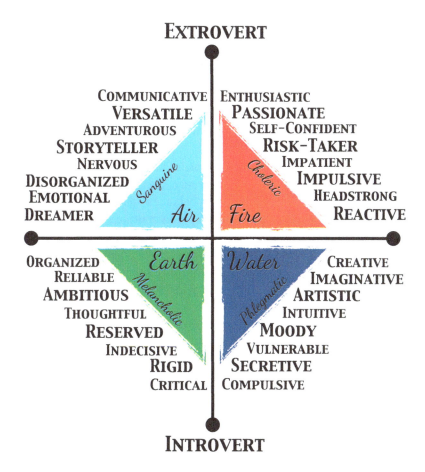

If we are Fiery persons, we are won by quiet explanation of reasons and motives, whereas by harsh commands we become embittered, hardened, and driven to strong-headed resistance. If we are Earthy persons, we are made suspicious and reticent by a rude word or an unfriendly encounter, whereas by continuous kind treatment, on the contrary, we are made pliable, trusting, affectionate. As a Fiery person, we can be relied upon, but with as an Airy person, others can hardly count even upon our apparently serious promises.

Without a knowledge of our temperament and that of others, we will treat them often wrongly, to their and to our own disadvantage.

With a knowledge of our temperaments, we bear more patiently with others. If we know that their defects are the consequence of their temperament, we excuse them more readily and will not so easily be excited or angered by them. We remain quiet, for instance, even if a Fiery is severe, sharp-edged, impetuous, or obstinate. If an Earthy person is slow, hesitating, undecided; if he does not speak much and even if he says awkwardly the little we have to say; or if an Airy person is very talkative, light-minded, and frivolous; if a Watery cannot be aroused from our usual indifference, we do not become irritated.

It is of the greatest benefit, furthermore to recognize fully our own temperament. Only if we know it can we judge our self correctly—our moods, our peculiarities, our past life.

If we know our own temperament, we can work out our own completion and perfection with greater assurance, because the whole effort toward self-perfection consists in attaining balance and in the combating our imbalances. Thus, as the Fiery, we will have to conquer, in the first place, our obstinacy, our anger, our pride; as the Earthy, our lack of courage and our dread of suffering; as the Airy, our talkativeness, our inconsistency; as the Watery, our laziness, our lack of energy. If we know our self, we will become more humble, realizing that many good traits, which we considered to be balanced, are merely good dispositions and the natural result of our temperament, rather than acquired characteristics.

Consequently, as the Fiery, we will judge more humbly of our strong will, our energy, and our fearlessness; as the Airy, of our cheerfulness, of our ability to get along well with difficult persons; as the Earthy, we will judge more humbly about our sympathy for others, about our love for solitude; as the Watery, about our good nature and our repose of mind.

The temperament is innate in each of us. Therefore it cannot be exchanged for another temperament. But we can and must cultivate and perfect the balanced elements of our temperament and combat and eradicate the imbalanced ones. Every temperament is in itself good. It is, therefore, ungrateful to wish to have another temperament.

Persons of various temperaments who live together should learn not to oppose but to support and supplement one another.

WHAT IS YOUR TEMPERAMENT?

Avicenna Cuisine begins with the Seven Nature-Given Essentials. With this system, we assume that all natural creations are composed of the four elemental qualities of hot, cold, wet and dry. However, this "does not mean that the number of elements in nature are four. In fact, they represent the basic division of matter, which is found in the universe."[3]

Temperament can be defined as: "the quality, which is produced, by actions and reactions of opposite qualities of elements, which are broken in smaller particles in order to facilitate the mixing of all particles. When those components interact among themselves by virtue of their respective powers (qualities), a condition is produced, which is found in equal proportions in all components of the elements."[4]

Another definition would be: Temperament is: "the pattern of inclinations that proceed from the physiological constitution of the individual. It is a dynamic factor that takes into account the way that the individual will react to stimuli of various kinds."[5]

Due to the fact that our temperament is rooted in our physiological structure, it is something innate within us. It is that within us which makes us each a unique individual. We are able to modify our innate temperament through the life style that we choose, but we never completely change it. We simply develop greater understanding of our individual personality, constitution or temperament as all mean basically the same thing. It is important to note, however, that we are never 100% one temperament or another. Rather, one temperament is dominant within each of us or why we show certain predominant characteristics of a particular temperament in order to better understand who we are. If we were to have a bit of all four temperaments and we were to take the best of each, as an Airy person we would have a generous heart, be sympathetic and full of life. Being part Fiery, we would show unending energy and persistence; being part Watery we would have self-control and be cautious; and, finally, being a bit Earthy, we would have a depth of feeling.

THE FOUR BALANCED TEMPERAMENTS

BALANCED TEMPERAMENTS

Balanced-tempered types are Air-Earth, Earth-Air, Fire-Water, and Water-Fire. Each of these temperament combinations possesses all four elemental qualities of hot, cold, wet, and dry. When one has all four elemental qualities in the right proportions, then this is considered equitable in terms of quantity and quality. Whereas in the other temperaments you will learn about next, the temperament is not balanced, but leans towards one or both of the opposite qualities. For instance, between hot and cold, or wet and dry. After taking the Avicenna Cuisine Temperament Test and receiving results indicating you have a balanced temperament, you should follow the same Nurturing Essentials as listed for the primary Air, Fire, Earth, or Water temperament, while also maintaining your current diet.

THE TWELVE OTHER TEMPERAMENTS

CHAPTER 17

How to Determine Your Temperament

ACCORDING TO AVICENNA CUISINE, OUR temperament, held together by our humours, combines our physical, mental, emotional and spiritual characteristics that then determine the way we feel, act and think.

We are born with a particular temperament or natural, innate disposition that develops from our humours. This inherent temperament includes the Seven Nature-Given Essentials as described above. These Seven Nature-Given Essentials depend upon the temperament of our parents, the time and place of our birth, our age and the climate in which we live, among other considerations.

Through our nurturing process and the Six Nurturing Essentials, our natural disposition changes somewhat over time. Each one of us is a unique individual and as such we each have a particular temperament and, at the same time, we share characteristics with others. Therefore, we need to determine our temperament and get to know ourselves better in order to craft a healthy diet that suits us best.

By taking the Temperament Test (see Chapter 23), you will have determined some aspects of your body-mind-energy Primary and possibly Secondary Imbalanced Temperament. As we have seen in the previous chapter, according to Avicenna Cuisine, a person's temperament is influenced by the equity of the elemental qualities that form the humours in our blood at conception.

The four temperaments have been given different names in English. When referring just to temperament without recognizing its origin in the humours and relating it only to physical-psychological characteristics, it is called Sanguine, Choleric, Phlegmatic or Melancholic. With Avicenna Cuisine, in order to make a distinction that the temperament being referred to here traces its origins back to the humours, we have used the following:

- Airy: (hot and wet, blood humour, salty, the physical-psychological temperament, also known as "Sanguine")

- Fiery: (hot and dry, yellow bile humour, bitter, the physical-psychological temperament, also known as "Choleric")
- Watery: (cold and wet, phlegmatic humour, sweet, the physical-psychological temperament, also known as "Phlegmatic")
- Earthy: (cold and dry, black bile or melancholic humour, sour, the physical-psychological temperament, also known as "Melancholic")

It is important to repeat that all four humours are found in our blood and that our blood itself is one of the four humours. Hot and cold are primary or active qualities. Hot-tempered foods stimulate our metabolism while cold-tempered foods quiet our metabolism and relieve our body of excess heat. Wet and dry are passive qualities. Wet-tempered foods are moistening, while dry-tempered foods help in evacuating excess fluids from our bodies.

Our bodies develop an imbalanced temperament when we consume food or drink that changes or transforms our humours. All imbalances of our humours develop during the digestive process. We have seen how the digestive process is regulated by our Natural Drive located in our liver. It is our liver that receives the chyme from the digestive process in our stomach.

According to Avicenna, our temperament arises from the humours and this determines the way in which we function. Every animal and every one of its organs have the most appropriate and the best adapted temperament for its various functions. Some have been made more hot, others more cold, others drier and more moister.

Our temperament is "equable" when the contrary qualities are in perfect equilibrium and out of harmony or "imbalanced" when our temperament tends toward a particular quality. An imbalanced temperament, or humour from the elemental qualities, determines our susceptibility to particular illnesses as well as our behavior and emotional inclinations. Healing, then, is based on the principle of opposites. That is, "cold" diseases can be healed by "hot" remedies and vice versa.

There are twelve types of temperaments as seen in the previous graphic. The top four are the simple temperaments. A simple temperament may change into a compound one. The bottom eight are where the elemental qualities of one primary temperament are shared with another. For example, a primary Airy temperament and secondary Fiery temperament share heat and so on.

Questions to Consider to Determine Your Temperament

- Do I react immediately and vehemently or slowly and superficially to a strong impression made upon me?
- Am I inclined to act at once or to remain calm and to wait?
- Does the excitement last for a long time or only for a short while?

Another very practical way to determine our temperament consists in considering our reactions to offenses, by asking these questions:

- Can I forgive when offended?
- Do I bear grudges and resent insults?

If one must answer: usually I cannot forget insults, I brood over them. To think of them excites me anew. I can bear a grudge a long time, several days, even weeks if somebody has offended me. I try to evade those who have offended me, refuse to speak to them, etc., then, one is either of Fiery or Earthy temperament.

If on the contrary the answer is: I do not harbor ill will. I cannot be angry with anybody for a long time. I forget even actual insults very soon. Sometimes I decide to show anger, but I cannot do so, at least not for a long time, at most an hour or two. If such is the answer, then we are either Airy or Watery.

After having recognized that one is of the Fiery or Earthy temperament the following questions should be answered:

- Am I quickly excited at offenses?
- Do I manifest my resentment by words or action?
- Do I feel inclined to oppose an insult immediately and retaliate?
- Or, do I remain calm outwardly at offenses received in spite of internal excitement?
- Am I frightened by offenses, disturbed, despondent, so that I do not find either the right words or the courage for a reply, and therefore, remain silent?
- Does it happen repeatedly that I hardly feel the offense at the moment when I receive it, but a few hours later, or even the following day, feel it so much more keenly?

In the first case, the person is Fiery; in the second, Earthy.

Upon ascertaining that our temperament is either Airy or Watery one must inquire further:

- Am I suddenly inflamed with anger at offenses received?
- Do I feel inclined to flare up and to act rashly?
- Or, do I remain quiet?
- Indifferent?
- Am I not easily swayed by my feelings?
  In the first case we are Airy, in the second, Watery.

It is very important, and indeed necessary to determine, first of all, our basic temperament by answering these questions, to be able to refer the various symptoms of the different temperaments to their proper source. Only then can self-knowledge be deepened to a full realization of how far the various light and dark sides of our temperament are developed, and of the modifications and variations our predominant temperament may have undergone by mixing with another temperament.

It is usually considered very difficult to recognize our own temperament or that of another person. Experience, however, teaches that with proper guidance, most persons can quite easily learn to know their own temperament, and that of their friends.

Greater difficulties, however, arise in discovering the temperament in the following instances:

- As an Airy person, who by nature is very much inclined to live in peace and harmony with others, we can become very annoying and cause great trouble by giving way to envy and anger.
- As an Earthy-tempered individual, we never allow our naturally sad, morose, discouraging temperament to show itself.

We only possess only slight knowledge of our self. We neither recognize our balanced nor imbalanced temperament, nor do we understand the intensity of our own evil inclinations and the degree of our excitability. Consequently we will not have a clear idea of our temperament. If anyone tries to assist us to know our self by questioning us, we gives false answers, not intentionally, but simply because we do not know our self.

We are very nervous. The signs of nervousness, as restlessness, irritability, inconstancy of humor and resolution, our inclination to melancholy and discouragement, manifest themselves so forcibly within us that the symptoms of temperament are more or less obscured.

We have a mixed temperament. It will be a great help in such cases to know the temperaments of the parents of such a person. If the father and mother are of the same temperament, the children will probably inherit the temperament of the parents. If the father and mother are of a Fiery temperament, the children will also be Fiery. If, however, the father and mother are of different temperaments, the children will inherit the different temperaments. If, for instance, the father is of a Fiery temperament and the mother Earthy, the children will be either Fiery with an Earthy mixture, or Earthy with a Fiery tendency, according to the degree of influence of either of the two parents.

In order to learn the predominant temperament, it is absolutely necessary to follow closely the above-mentioned questions concerning the temperaments. But it also happens, although not so often as many believe, that in one-person, two temperaments are so mixed that both are equally strong.

In this case it is naturally very hard to judge with which temperament the respective person is to be classified. It is probable, however, that in the course of time, when facing difficulties, one of the temperaments will manifest itself predominantly.

A very valuable help for the discernment of the mixed, and especially of the pure temperaments are the expression of the eye and more or less the manner in which a person walks. The eye of the Fiery is resolute, firm, energetic, fiery. The eye of the Airy is cheerful, friendly, and careless. The eye of the Earthy looks more or less sad and troubled. The eye of the Watery is faint, devoid of expression.

The Fiery steps up firmly, resolutely, is more or less always in a hurry. The Airy is light-footed and quick; their walking is often like dancing. The gait of the Earthy is slow and heavy while that of the Watery is lazy and sluggish.

CHAPTER 18

AIRY TEMPERAMENT
Humour: **BLOOD**
Basic Qualities: Hot and Wet

The Characteristics of the Airy Temperament

As Airy persons, we are quickly aroused and vehemently excited by whatever influences us. The reaction follows immediately, but the impression lasts but a short time. Consequently the remembrance of the impression does not easily cause new excitement.

The Airy Temperament:

1   We are self-composed; we seldom shows signs of embarrassment, perhaps forward or bold.
2   We are eager to express self before a group; we like to be heard.
3   We prefer group activities, work or play, and are not easily satisfied with individual projects.
4   We are not insistent upon acceptance of our ideas or plans; we agree readily with others' wishes; we are compliant and yielding.
5   We are good in details; we prefer activities requiring pep and energy.
6   We are impetuous and impulsive; our decisions are often wrong.
7   We are keenly alive to environment, physical and social.
8   We tend to take success for granted and are followers who may lack initiative.
9   Hearty and cordial, even to strangers, we form acquaintances easily.
10 We tend to elation of spirit and not given to worry and anxiety.
11 We seek a wide and broad range of friendships and are not selective;

nor exclusive in games.

12   We are quick and decisive in movements and have a pronounced or excessive energy output.

13   We turn from one activity to another in rapid succession with little perseverance.

14   We make adjustments easily, welcome changes and make the best appearance possible.

15   We are frank, talkative, sociable, readily expressing our emotions; we do not stand on ceremony.

16   We have frequent fluctuations of mood and tend to frequent alterations of elation and depression

The Fundamental Disposition of the Airy Temperament

Superficiality

We do not penetrate the depth, the essence of things. We do not embrace the whole, but are satisfied with the superficial and with a part of the whole. Before we have mastered one subject, our interest relaxes because new impressions have already captured our attention. We love light work that attracts attention, where there is no need of deep thought, or great effort. To be sure, it is hard to convince us that we are superficial. On the contrary, we imagine that we have grasped the subject wholly and perfectly.

Our decisions are likely to be wrong because our inquiry into things is only superficial and partial. We do not see difficulties. We are inclined to partiality because of our feelings of sympathy. Our undertakings fail easily because we always take success for granted, as a matter of course, and, therefore, do not give sufficient attention to possible obstacles. Also, we lack perseverance and our interest in things fades quickly.

Instability

Because the impressions made upon us do not last, we are easily followed by others. The consequence is a great instability that must be taken into account by anyone who deals with us, if that person does not wish to be disappointed.

We are unstable in the pursuit of balance. We permit others to lead us and are, therefore easily led astray if we fall into the hands of unscrupulous persons. Our enthusiasm is quickly aroused for the attaining balance, but it also vanishes quickly.

We are always changing our moods. We can quickly pass from tears to laughter and vice versa. We are fickle in our views. Today we may defend what we vehemently opposed a week ago. We are unstable in our resolutions. If a new point of view presents itself we may readily upset the plans that we have made previously. Our inconsistency often causes people to think that we have no character, that we are not guided by principles. We naturally deny such charges, because we always find a reason for our changes. We forget that it is necessary to consider everything well and to look into and investigate everything carefully beforehand in order not to be captivated by every new idea or mood. We are also inconsistent at our work or entertainment. We love variety in everything. We resemble a bee which flies from flower to flower or the child who soon tires of the new toy.

TENDENCY TO THE EXTERNAL

We do not like to enter into our "self," but direct our attention to the external. In our respect we are the very opposite of the Earthy person who is given to introspection, who prefers to be absorbed by deep thoughts and more or less ignores the external. Our leaning to the external is shown in the keen interest that we pay to our own appearance, as well as to that of others—to a beautiful face, to fine and modern clothes, and to good manners. The five senses are especially active within us, while the Fiery uses reason and will and the Earthy, feelings. As the Airy type, we see everything, hear everything, and talk about everything. Because of our vivacity, we have an eye for details, an advantageous disposition that is more or less lacking in Fiery and Earthy persons. Our self-knowledge is deficient because we always cater to the external and is loath to enter into our inner self and give deeper thought to our own actions.

OPTIMISM

We look at everything from the bright side. We are optimistic, overlook difficulties, and are always sure of success. If we fail, we do not worry about it too long but console our self easily. Our vivacity explains our inclination to poke fun at others, to tease them and to play tricks on them. We take it for granted that others are willing to take such things in good humor and we are very much surprised if they are vexed on account of our mockery or improper jokes.

Many things which cause someone else a great deal of anxiety and trouble do not affect us in the least, because we are optimists and as such overlook difficulties and prefer to look at affairs from the sunny side. Even if we are occasionally exasperated and sad, we soon find our balance again. Our sadness does not last long, but gives way quickly to happiness. Our sunny quality helps us to find community life much easier and to overcome the difficulties of such life more readily than do Fiery or Earthy persons. We can get along well even with persons generally difficult to work with.

THE DARK SIDE OF THE AIRY TEMPERAMENT

ABSENCE OF DEEP PASSIONS

Our passions are quickly excited, but they do not make a deep and lasting impression. We may be compared to a straw fire, which flares up suddenly, but just as quickly dies down, while the passions of a Fiery are to be compared to a raging, all-devouring conflagration. We are noted for our facility and vivacity of speech, our inexhaustible variety of topics and flow of words that often make us disagreeable to others. When imbalanced, we tend to babble and be indecisive, even a bit eccentric. We often tend to talk our "self" through whatever it is that we are feeling rather than allowing our self to experience our real emotions or we analyze the situation without regard for the emotional feeling it has brought about within us.

VANITY AND SELF-COMPLACENCY

Our pride does not manifest itself as inordinate ambition or obstinacy, as it does if we are Fiery, nor as fear of humiliation if we are Earthy, but as a strong inclination to vanity and self-complacency. We find a childish joy and satisfaction in our outward appearance, in our clothes and work. We love to look at our "self" in the mirror. We feel happy when praised and are, therefore, very susceptible to flattery. By praise and flattery we can easily be seduced to perform the most difficult tasks.

INCLINATION TO FLIRTATION, JEALOUSY AND ENVY

We are inclined to inordinate intimacy and flirtation because we lack deep spirituality and lean to the external and are willing to accept flatteries. However, our love is not deep and changes easily. We are pliable and docile. The virtue of obedience, which is generally considered as difficult, is easy for us. As an otherwise well-trained Airy, we would be content with superficial familiarities as tokens of affection, but in consequence of our levity and readiness to yield, as well as on account of our optimistic beliefs, we can be easily led to the most grievous quirks.

Vanity and tendency to love affairs lead us to jealousy, envy, and to all the petty, mean, and detestable faults that are usually the consequence of envy. Because we are easily influenced by exterior impressions or feelings of sympathy or antipathy, it is hard for us to be impartial and just. We are greatly inclined to flatter those whom we love.

INORDINATE LOVE OF PLEASURE

We do not like to be alone. We love company and amusement. We want to enjoy life. We can be very frivolous in our amusements.

DREAD OF STRUGGLING FOR BALANCE
IF IT REQUIRES STRENUOUS EFFORTS

Everything that requires the denial of the gratification of the senses is very hard on us. For instance, for us to guard our eyes, ears, and tongue to keep silence. We do not like to deny our self some favorite food or drink.

BRIGHT SIDE OF THE AIRY TEMPERAMENT

We have many qualities on account of which we fare well with our fellow human beings and endear our self to them.

COMMUNICATORS

We are extroverts. We easily make acquaintance with other people, are very communicative, chatty, and associate easily with strangers. We are friendly in our speech and behavior and can pleasantly entertain others by our interesting narratives and witticisms. We are very pleasant and willing to oblige. We dispense our acts of kindness not so coldly as a Fiery, not so warmly and touchingly as the Earthy, but at least in such a jovial and pleasant way that we are graciously received. We have a remarkable faculty of drawing the attention of others to their faults without causing immediate and great displeasure. We do not find it hard to correct others. If it is necessary to inform someone of bad news, it is well to assign us to that task. We are candid and can easily make known our difficulties. We tend to easily communicate, are quick-witted and easily adapt to various circumstances and situations. As an Airy-tempered person, we tend to be storytellers, translators and journalists as we excel at communications. We are great networkers.

COMPASSIONATE

We are compassionate whenever a mishap befalls our neighbor and are always ready to cheer him by a friendly remark. If we are an Airy-tempered person, we love human kind and are oriented towards being very social. Relationship centered, we tend to be cooperative, balanced and initiate new ideas.

FORGIVING

We are quickly excited by an offense and may show our anger violently and at times imprudently, but as soon as we have given vent to our wrath, we are again pleasant and bear no grudge. We do not dwell long over unpleasant happenings.

METHODS OF SELF-TRAINING THE AIRY TEMPERAMENT

- In regard to life, we must continually bear in mind that we need to continue thinking about what we are doing. We must consider every point, anticipate all possible difficulties. We must not be overconfident, over optimistic.
- We must guard the palate against overindulging in exquisite foods and drinks.
- We must absolutely see to it that we be influenced by the good and not by the bad, that we accept counsel and direction.
- We must continually struggle against those faults to which we are so much inclined by our natural disposition, such as, vanity and self-complacency; love of particular friendships; sentimentality; sensuality; jealousy; levity; superficiality and instability.

SPECIAL CONSIDERATIONS IN BALANCING THE AIRY TEMPERAMENT

Educating us is comparatively easy. We must be looked after. We must be told that we are not allowed to leave our work unfinished. Our assertions, resolutions, and promises must not be taken too seriously. We must continually be checked as to whether we have really executed our work carefully. Flatteries must not be accepted from us and especially constant guard must be kept in case any preference be shown to us on account of our affable disposition. It must be remembered that we will not keep to our self what we are told or what we notice about anyone. It is advisable to think twice before taking us into confidence.

Airy-tempered people are less practical than the Earthy type, but certainly more practical than the Watery or Fiery-tempered person. If we fail to focus on the goals that we have set, we may become detached from them, developing into being dreamers and procrastinators. We are fair-minded and try to consider the view of others in our conversations.

Just as air is everywhere, as Airy-tempered people we are concerned with thinking, relating and communicating. We live for exchanging ideas with others and cherish our personal interactions with others.

In the education of Airy children, the following points should be observed:

- They must be consistently taught to practice self-denial, especially by subduing the senses. Perseverance at work and observance of order must be continually insisted upon.
- They must be kept under strict supervision and guidance. They must be carefully guarded against bad company, because they can so easily be seduced.
- Leave them their cheerfulness and let them have their fun, only guard them against overdoing it.

ACTIONS BASED ON THE
SEVEN NATURE-GIVEN ESSENTIALS

THE ELEMENTS

The Element of Air is associated with the signs Gemini, Libra and Aquarius, and it also symbolizes the natural third, seventh and eleventh houses in astrology.

Being Airy as well as having planets in the Air signs, we use our thinking abilities to try to make sense of our lives.

The Airy temperament is based on the classical element of Air that is hot and wet. Air is light. It infuses all that is on the earth. There is air in the atmosphere around us as well as in deep, cavernous caves. Air is light and it rises. It is as difficult to control as fire so it wants to be free while at the same time, linking one thing to another. "Air is associated with words and language. Language and words are essentially verbal, and speech requires air. It has a serial quality. You can blow air from one position to another. For example, you can direct the breath to blow away some dust—the air moves from the mouth to the position of the dust."[6]

THE HUMOURS

As we have noted, an Airy Temperament is associated with our blood humour. We Aires are typically a balanced, fair and just person who is thoughtful and active in a consistent way We are good at judging people and situations while at the same time we do have mood shifts.[7]

PHYSIOLOGY

In terms of physiology, we Airy-tempered people stimulate our arteries and veins. Our hot and wet qualities give us our motivational energy. Many have observed that those of us who are Airy have "a good appetite, quick and good digestion, happy dreams and generally a happy nature."[8]

THE TEMPERAMENT

We have a tendency to action and being active. We rarely show that we are embarrassed by circumstances in which we find our self, but we respond with a certain boldness to the situation. External situations stimulate us to the extent that we prefer working with a group rather than alone. One of our major strengths is our attention to detail. We love learning and gaining new knowledge. If and when we succeed at a goal we have set, we put all our efforts into it. We lean towards being a follower instead of vying for a leadership position. We are not usually anxious, but rather carefree and cheerful. We easily adapt to new circumstances and make the best of it. We love to talk and express ourselves. We get along with others, even people who are considered to be hard to get along with.[9]

THE BREATH OF LIFE AND INNATE HEAT AS ENERGY GIVERS

The breath of we Airy types relates to our love of freedom. When we imagine our Airy self, we can feel the wind running through our hair and savor its freshness. We can imagine flying through it. When we inhale, we feel light. When we exhale we reach out to the air around and beyond us.[10]

THE ORGANS

As an Airy type, we have been found to develop yeast infections, as well as suffer from fatigue and high nervous energy because of our over indulgence in sugar and bread. While these two ingredients increase our energy level when we feel down, we continue to use them even when we have attained balance. When we learn to maintain a balance in what we consume, we will suffer less with physical problems. Studies have shown that when we tend to be absent to our "self," someone should check our blood sugar level and adjust it accordingly.[11]

An Airy-tempered person may present amongst many others, the following signs:

- Occurrence of headache
- Trembling lips
- Feeling of weakness occasionally and moreover weakening of the limbs
- Swollen tongue
- Nose itching
- Cracked nails
- Loose teeth

- Coughing
- Hemorrhoids
- Swollen liver

THE DIGESTIVE ASSISTANT DRIVES

As the Airy elemental qualities of hot and wet control our Digestive Assistants, we Airy-tempered individuals are prone to excess in appetite. We can over consume fatty, sweet and rich foods that place stress on our liver and possible digestive putrefaction. We need to concentrate on eating light and easy to digest foods.

At the dinner table, our type typically eats everything in sight. When we go to a restaurant, we end up talking so much that we forget to check out the menu before the waiter arrives. Studies have shown that stimulants such as Coffee, Sugar, Prescription Drugs and possibly Meat Products and Wheat are unsuitable for us. It has been said that we should eat: "greens daily in the form of Swiss Chard, Parsley, Mint, Coriander, Chives, Rocket Plant, Dark Greens, and Dark Green Lettuce, and avoid rich or sugary foods."[12]

HOW TO MANAGE AN AIRY TEMPERAMENT
- Concentrate on joy and joyous occasions with lots of fun time.
- Give much overt attention and display of love and affection.
- Spend quality time with them.
- Allow them to entertain or volunteer, making sure that they do not over extend themselves.
- When details become overwhelming show them sympathy.[13]

Primary

Sanguine
Air
Hot & Wet

Overview

Temperamental quality of Air.
Overall dominant qualities of **HEAT AND WETNESS.**
Any change in the ideal level of heat and wetness,
especially an increase in these qualities will negatively
affect you.

Personality:

- Strong Extrovert
- Enthusiastic
- Communicative
- Versatile
- Adventurous
- Storyteller
- Nervous
- Disorganized
- Emotional
- Dreamer

Increase In Heat & Wetness Can Be A Result Of:

- Hot and Wet Tempered Foods
- Very Hot Weather
- Summer Heat and Humidity
- Excessive Anger
- Lack of Sleep
- Vigorous Exercise

APPETITE The epicure. A craving for rich gourmet foods. Typically quite hearty.

DIGESTION Good to moderate digestion, but can be overwhelmed by excessive food.

6 NURTURE-GIVEN ESSENTIALS FOR AIR PRIMARY

AIR & ENVIRONMENT	Fresh air and a cool, properly ventilated environment are most ideal. Avoid staying in a hot and moist environment for too long.
PHYSICAL REST & ACTIVITY	Inadequate rest and vigorous exercise should be avoided. Light weight training and aerobics for 15-20 minutes are the most suitable.
SLEEP & WAKEFULNESS	This temperament requires a good nights sleep of 6-7 hours.
EMOTIONS & AROMATHERAPY	Avoid extreme emotions of anger, excitability, and irritability as much as possible. This can be managed with breathing exercises and meditation.
RETENTION & EVACUATION	Drink plenty of water to avoid and eliminate excess heat, which will also help your kidney function regularly. A high fiber diet will help maintain regular bowel habits. Laxatives are also beneficial.
FOOD, DIET & DRINK	Eat mainly cold and dry foods and occasionally cold and wet foods. Eat less hot and dry foods, and the least amount of hot and wet foods.

What To Eat

Sanguine
Air
Hot & Wet

Meats & Fish

Dry Veggies

Dry Fruits

Spices & Herbs

Flour & Grains

Nuts & Seeds

Cooking Oils

Visit avicennacuisine.com for a full database of ingredients.

CHAPTER 19

FIERY TEMPERAMENT
Humour: Yellow Bile
Basic Qualities: Hot and Dry

The Characteristics of the Fiery Temperament

As Fiery-tempered persons, we are quickly and vehemently excited by any and every influence. Immediately the reaction sets in and the impression remains a long time. We have a great sense of enthusiasm. We are not satisfied with the ordinary, but aspire after great and lofty things. We crave great success in temporal affairs. We seek large fortunes, a vast business, an elegant home, a distinguished reputation or a predominant position. We aspire to the highest also in matters spiritual.

The Fiery Temperament:

1   We are insistent upon the acceptance of our ideas or plans; argumentative and persuasive.
2   Impetuous and impulsive, we plunge into situations where forethought would have deterred us.
3   We are very sensitive and easily hurt.
4   We have a marked tendency to persevere.
5   We do not abandon something readily regardless of success.
6   We react strongly to praise or blame.
7   Other than anger, our emotions are not freely or spontaneously expressed.
8   We may be conceited and resort to hypocrisy, deceit, disguise.

THE FUNDAMENTAL DISPOSITION OF THE FIERY TEMPERAMENT

The natural characteristic of the Fiery-tempered is ambition. Our desire to excel and succeed. We despise the little and vulgar and, rather, aspires to the noble and heroic. In our aspiration for great things, we are supported by the following characteristics:

A KEEN INTELLECT

We are not always, but usually endowed with considerable intelligence. We are persons of reason while our imagination and our emotions are poor and stunted.

A STRONG WILL

We are not frightened by difficulties, but in case of obstacles show our energy so much the more and persevere also under great difficulties until we have reached our goal. We are unlikely to develop despondency. We are very stubborn and opinionated. We think we are always right, want to have the last word, tolerate no contradiction, and are never willing to give in.

STRONG PASSIONS

We are very passionate. Whenever we are bent upon carrying out our plans or finds opposition, we are filled with passionate excitement.

WISH TO DOMINATE

Often times we have a subconscious impulse to dominate others and make them subservient. We have been created to rule. We feel happy when we are in a position to command, to draw others to us and to organize large groups. We are domineering and inordinately ambitious. We want to hold the first place, to be admired by others, to subject others to our self. We belittle, combat, and even persecute by unfair means those who dare to oppose our ambition.

THE DARK SIDE OF THE FIERY TEMPERAMENT

HASTY

A very great impediment in our yearning for great things is our imprudent haste. We are immediately and totally absorbed by the aim we have in mind and rush for our goal with great haste and impetuosity. We consider but too little whether we can really reach our goal. We see only one road, the one we in our impetuosity have taken without sufficient consideration. We do not notice that by another road we could reach our goal more easily. By our imprudence we waste a great deal of our energy, which could be used to better advantage. We irritate our friends, so that finally we stand almost alone and are disliked by most people. We deprive our self of our best successes, even though we will not admit that we are the main cause of our failure. We show the same imprudence in selecting the means for the pursuit of perfection, so that in spite of great efforts we do not acquire it.

PROUD

If we meet great obstacles, because of our pride, we can hardly make up our mind to turn back, but instead we continue with great obstinacy on the original course. We dash our head against the wall rather than take notice of the door, which is right near and wide open.

CONCEITED

We tend to be full of our "self." We have a great opinion of our good qualities and our successful work and consider our self as something extraordinary and as one called upon to perform great feats. We consider even our very defects as being justified as if we deserve something great and worthy of praise, for instance, our pride, our obstinacy, and our anger. We have a great deal of self-confidence. We rely too much upon our own knowledge and ability. We refuse the help of others and prefer to work alone, partly because we do not like to ask for help, partly because we believe that we are more capable than others and are sure to succeed without the help of others.

EXTREMELY SENSITIVE

We feel deeply hurt when we are humiliated or put to shame. Even the recollection of it fills us with great displeasure because it has given us a lower opinion of ourselves.

ANGRY

Contradiction, resistance, and personal offenses vehemently excite us. Our excitement manifests itself in harsh words that may seem very decent and polite as far as phrasing is concerned, but hurt to the core by the tone in which they are spoken. Nobody can hurt our fellow human being with a few words more bitterly than we Fiery type. Things are made even worse by the fact that in our anger, we impetuosity make false and exaggerated reproaches, and may go so far in our passion as to misconstrue the intentions and to pervert the words of those who irritated us, thus, blaming with the sharpest of expressions, faults which in reality were not committed at all. By such injustice which we inflict in our anger upon our neighbor, we can offend and alienate even our best friends.

As the Fiery type, we may even indulge in furious outbursts of anger. Our anger easily degenerates into hatred. We cannot forget grievous offenses. In our anger and pride we permit our self to be drawn to actions that we know will be very detrimental to our self and to others. An example is that we would ruin our health, our work, our fortune, loss of our position, and complete rupture with intimate friends. By reason of our pride and anger we may totally ignore and cast aside the very plans for the realization of which we have worked for years.

DECEIT, DISGUISE AND HYPOCRISY

As noble and magnanimous as we are by nature, the tendency to pride and self-will may lead us to the deceit and hypocrisy. We practice deceit because we are in no way willing to concede that we succumbed to a weakness and suffered a defeat. We use hypocrisy, deception, and even outright lies, if we realize that we cannot carry out our plans by force.

LACK OF SYMPATHY

As the Fiery type, as said above, we are persons of reason. We have two heads but no heart. Our lack of human sentiment and sympathy is, in a way, of great advantage to us. Effeminate, sentimental dispositions are repugnant to us. We hate the caresses and sentimentality that arise between intimate friends. False sympathy cannot influence us to neglect our duties or abandon our principles. On the other hand, our lack of sympathy has great disadvantages. We can be extremely hard, heartless, and even cruel in regard to the sufferings of others. We can cold-bloodedly trample upon the welfare of others if we cannot otherwise reach our goal. We may tend to look down on our fellow man. To our mind others are ignorant, weak, unskilled, slow, at least when compared with our self. We show our contempt of our neighbor by despising, mocking, making belittling remarks about others and by our proud behavior toward those around him.

Bright Side of the Fiery Temperament

Great Energy

We have great energy and activity, a sharp intellect, strong and resolute will, good powers of concentration, constancy, magnanimity, and liberality.

Practical

We are practical rather than theoretical. We are more inclined to work than to think. Inactivity is repugnant to us, and we are always looking forward to the next labor or to the formulation of some great project. Once we have set upon a plan of work, we immediately set our hand to the task. Hence we produce many leaders.

Hard Working

We do not leave for tomorrow what we can do today, but sometimes we may try to do today what we should leave for tomorrow. If difficulties and obstacles arise, we immediately set about to overcome them and, although we often have strong movements of anger and impatience in the face of problems, once we have conquered these movements we acquire a tenderness and sweetness of disposition that are noteworthy.

If we develop our faculties and use them for good and noble purposes, we may do great things for the benefit of our fellow human beings. We are assisted by our sharp intellect, our enthusiasm for the noble and the great, the force and resolution of our will, which shrinks before no difficulty, and the keen vivacity which influences all our thoughts and plans.

SUCCESSFUL IN OUR PROFESSIONAL WORK

We are very successful also in our professional work. Being of an active temperament, we feel a continual inclination to activity and occupation. We cannot be without work, and we work quickly and diligently. In our enterprises we are persevering and full of courage in spite of obstacles. Without hesitation, we can be placed at difficult posts and everything can be entrusted to us. In our speech we are brief and definite. We abhor useless repetitions. Our brevity, positive attitude, firmness in speech and appearance gives us a great deal of authority, especially when engaged in educational work. As Fiery teachers, we have something virile about us. We do not allow affairs to get beyond our control, as is often the case with slow, irresolute, Earthy persons. A Fiery can keep a secret like a grave.

METHODS OF SELF-TRAINING OF THE FIERY TEMPERAMENT

- As Fiery-tempered persons, we need high ideals and great thoughts.
- We must work on our self day by day.
- We must, above all, keep one strong resolution in our mind: I will never seek myself, but on the contrary I will consider myself.
- We combat our pride and anger continually. Pride is the misfortune of we Fiery types, humility our only salvation. Therefore we should make it a point of our particular examination of conscience for years.
- We must humiliate ourselves voluntarily. For us it is better to permit others to humiliate him, than to humiliate ourselves.
- We must practice a true and trusting devotion to the humble.

SPECIAL CONSIDERATIONS IN BALANCING
THE FIERY TEMPERAMENT

As Fiery-tempered, we are capable of great benefit to our family and our surroundings. We are naturally the born and never discouraged leader and organizer. On the other hand, we can, if we do not control the weak side of our temperament, act as dynamite in private and public and cause great disturbance.

We should be well instructed so that we can apply our good talents to the best advantage. Otherwise, we will in the course of time pursue pet ideas to the neglect of our professional work, or what is worse, we will be very proud and conceited, although in reality we have not cultivated our faculties and is not, in fact, thorough.

We Fiery-tempered who are less talented or not sufficiently educated can make many mistakes once we are independent or have power to command as superiors. We are likely to make life bitter for those around us because we insist stubbornly upon the fulfillment of our orders, although we may not fully understand the affairs in question or may have altogether false ideas about them. As such, we often act according to the ill-famed motto: Thus I want it. Thus I command it. My will is sufficient reason.

We must be influenced to accept voluntarily and gladly what is done for the humiliation of our pride and the soothing of our anger. By hard, proud treatment we are not improved, but embittered and hardened, whereas even as a very proud Fiery we can easily be influenced to good by reasonable suggestions. In the training of we Fiery types, our teachers should never allow themselves to be carried away by anger nor should they ever give expression to the determination to 'break' our obstinacy. It is absolutely necessary to remain calm and to allow us time to 'cool off' and then to persuade us to accept guidance in order to correct our faults and bring out the good in us.

In training Fiery-tempered children:

- We must place high ideas before them.
- We should appeal to their good will, their sense of honor, their abhorrence of the vulgar.
- We should influence them to voluntarily correct their faults and develop our good qualities.
- Teachers should not embitter them by humiliating punishments, but try to show them the necessity and justice of the punishment inflicted; yet be firm in what is demanded.

ACTIONS BASED ON THE
SEVEN NATURE-GIVEN ESSENTIALS

THE ELEMENTS

The Fire Signs are Aries, Leo and Sagittarius and we represent the spirit in motion. We suddenly have flashes of insight and great bursts of energy as those of us with a Fiery temperament speak for the element of fire being hot and dry. Fire enlivens and quickens. It can add energy at the same time that it can consume and destroy. When we think about fire, we think of movement that calls for action. We are emotionally connected with desires while our thoughts and ideas are given life by our Fiery temperament. At the same time that we are inspired with new life and new ideas, our colder ideas are consumed by it along with our attachments and attitudes towards our ego. This means that our spiritual self is constantly like the phoenix arising from the ashes, burning the previous and giving birth to the next. Our Fiery temperament tends to burn the old and recreate the new as it purifies our "self," raising us towards the light and further inspirations and intuitions.[14]

THE HUMOURS

If we have a balanced Fiery-temper, our predominance of yellow bile humour causes us to be quick-tempered. We are quick at making decisions and are clear that we prefer action over contemplation. However, we have to be careful because an excess of yellow bile humour can become burned leading us to melancholia and negativity, being quick to anger and perhaps even occasionally becoming enraged.[15]

PHYSIOLOGY

Physiologically, our Fiery temperament is closely associated with our nervous system, acting to increase the rate at which it functions. It has a warming effect on the body, stimulates our intellect, and increases our physical and mental activity and courage. Its receptacle is the gall bladder. Signs of excess yellow bile humour are: leanness of body; hollow eyes; anger without a cause; a testy disposition; yellowness of the skin; bitterness in the throat; pricking pains in the head; a swifter and stronger pulse than typical; troublesome sleep; and dreams of fire, lightning, anger and/or fighting.[16]

THE TEMPERAMENT

As Fiery-tempered, we are highly reactive in a positive or active sense. We tend to go towards extremes more easily. Our emotions are more on the surface and tend toward extroversion being the extroverts that we are. We identify with the personality we perceive. We are also changeable, so we can consume that attachment to one personality and shift toward another—as the candle flame passes one wick to another or the flames of a forest fire go from tree to tree.[17]

The Breath of Life and Innate Heat as Energy Givers

Being of the Fiery temperament, our breath is quickening. Our breath sparks inspiration. When we inhale, we can come in touch with our desire to be authentic, to lead a meaningful life and to stand up for whatever it is in which we believe. When we exhale, we feel that we are radiating light, offering up the parts of ourselves that we want to transform. "Subject our self-doubt, cynicism, addictive patterns or resentments to the fire. Avoid making pledges we will not keep. Simply clarify our intention and open our self to the purification process. Instead of using will power to change, we need to use our Fiery temperament as a teacher who burns what needs to be burned and changes and grows that which we want by taping into our natural Fiery energies."[18]

The Organs

When we have an excess of yellow bile humour, it indicates that there is an excess of heat and dryness in our body. It can result in headaches, difficulty sleeping and excessive appetite. As Fiery types, we may experience "problems with anxiety, agitation, frenzy, nervous exhaustion, and insomnia. We may also have palpitations, hypoglycemia, rashes, palsy, or strokes."[19]

The Digestive Assistant Drives

If we are Fiery-tempered, we have a good digestive process and are basically able to digest foods and drinks quickly. Even after eating a large meal, we may be hungry again in an hour. As our metabolism works swiftly, we do not usually gain a great deal of weight. We may crave salty and spicy foods, but we should hold back eating them because they tend to cause an imbalance. We need to eat a moderate amount and not cave into our seemingly limitless appetite.

As a Fiery-tempered person, we seldom vary our menu from one day to another. While eating, we swallow our food in large chunks, talking while we are chewing. Beneficial foods for our type are those that moisturize and cool such as liquids, fruit juices and vegetables, warm soups, denser root vegetables, sea vegetables, legumes, and fish protein. Raw and cooked foods can be used to balance our hyper or hypo activity. Warm, cooked foods are stimulating when we have slowed down and are tired. On the other hand, cool, raw foods are beneficial when they are overexcited.[20]

How to Manage a Fiery Temperament

- Express joy at their achievements and contributions even if we receive a response of indifference.
- Tell them they have done well when they have done so.
- Be loyal to them. Criticism or sarcasm is seen as a lack of loyalty.
- Challenge the Fiery to be more compassionate by being able to walk in another person's shoes. Help them express appreciation even if there is no agreement on their part, because agreement involves a judgment about results.
- Help them to learn to appreciate relationships by developing compassion, and encouragement of others as well as listening to others in a non-judgmental way and not just concentrating on results.
- Assist them in unwinding.[21]

OVERVIEW

Temperamental quality of Fire.
Overall dominant qualities of **HEAT AND DRYNESS.**
Any change in the ideal level of heat and dryness,
especially an increase in these qualities will negatively
affect you.

PERSONALITY:

- Industrious
- Capable
- Goal-Oriented
- Detailed
- Attentive
- Competitive
- Forceful
- Sarcastic
- Hostile
- Perfectionist

INCREASE IN HEAT & DRYNESS CAN BE A RESULT OF:

- Hot and Dry Tempered Foods
- Hot Weather
- Summer Heat
- Excessive Anger
- Lack of Sleep
- Irregular Bowel Movements
- Vigorous Exercise

APPETITE Carnivore, enjoys fried, salty or spicy foods. Craves intense or stimulating taste sensations.

DIGESTION Able to digest everything quickly when balanced and healthy. There's a tendency to have gastritis, hyperacidity and acid reflux.

6 NURTURE-GIVEN ESSENTIALS FOR FIRE PRIMARY

AIR & ENVIRONMENT	Fresh air and a cool, properly ventilated environment are most ideal. Over exposure to the sun or very hot climates should be avoided.
PHYSICAL REST & ACTIVITY	Exercise in the early morning or late in the evening. Avoid over excessive movements and vigorous exercises.
SLEEP & WAKEFULNESS	This temperament requires a good nights sleep of 6-8 hours as it is difficult to get adequate sleep. Resting for 45 minutes after lunch is also beneficial.
EMOTIONS & AROMATHERAPY	Avoid extreme emotions of anger, excitability, and irritability as much as possible. This can be managed with breathing exercises and meditation.
RETENTION & EVACUATION	Drink plenty of water to avoid and eliminate excess heat and toxins. Laxatives are also beneficial.
FOOD, DIET & DRINK	Eat mainly cold and wet foods and occasionally cold and dry foods. Eat less hot and wet foods and the least amount of hot and dry foods.

WHAT TO EAT *Choleric* **Fire** Hot & Dry	MEATS & FISH
WET VEGGIES	WET FRUITS
SPICES & HERBS	FLOUR & GRAINS
NUTS & SEEDS	COOKING OILS

Visit avicennacuisine.com for a full database of ingredients.

CHAPTER 20

EARTHY TEMPERAMENT
Humour: Black Bile
Basic Qualities: Cold and Dry

The Characteristics of the Earthy Temperament

As Earthy-tempered persons, we are but feebly excited by whatever acts upon us. The reaction is weak, but our feeble impression remains for a long time. Subsequently, similar impressions grow stronger and at last excite the mind so vehemently that it is difficult to eradicate it. Such impression may be compared to a post, which by repeated strokes is driven deeper and deeper into the ground, so that at last it is hardly possible to pull it out again. Our propensity needs special attention. It serves as a key to solve the many riddles in our behavior.

The Earthy Temperament:

1 We are self-conscious, easily embarrassed, timid, bashful.
2 We avoid talking before a group; when obliged to, we find it difficult
3 We prefer to work and play alone; we are good in details, careful.
4 We are deliberative and slow in making decisions, perhaps even over-cautious in minor matters.
5 We lack self-confidence and initiative; we are compliant and yielding.
6 We tend to detach ourselves from the environment and are reserved and distant, except to intimate friends.
7 We tend to depression and are frequently moody or gloomy as well as being very sensitive and easily hurt.
8 We do not form acquaintances readily, but prefer a narrow range of friends as we tend to exclude others.

9   We worry over possible misfortune and cross bridges before coming to them.

10   We are secretive, shut in and not inclined to speak unless spoken to.

11   We are slow in movement, deliberative or perhaps indecisive with frequent and constant moods.

12   We often represent ourselves at a disadvantage and we are modest and unassuming.

The Fundamental Disposition
of the Earthy Temperament

Inclination to Reflection

The thinking of the Earthy type easily turns into reflection. Our thoughts are far reaching. We dwell with pleasure upon the past and are preoccupied by occurrences of the long ago. We are penetrating and not satisfied with the superficial. We search for the cause and correlation of things. We seek laws that affect human life, the principles according to which we should act. Our thoughts are of a wide range. We look ahead into the future. We are of an extremely softhearted disposition. Our very thoughts arouse our own sympathy. Often they stir us up profoundly, particularly plans that we cherish, yet we hardly permit our fierce excitement to be noticed outwardly. If we are untrained, we are easily given to brooding and to daydreaming.

Love of Solitude

We do not feel at home among a crowd for any length of time. We love silence and solitude. Being inclined to introspection, we seclude our self from the crowds, forget our environment, and make poor use of our senses—eyes, ears, etc. In company, we are often distracted, because we are absorbed by our own thoughts. By reason of our lack of observation and our dreaming we have many a mishap in our daily life and at our work.

Serious Conception of Life

We look at life always from the serious side. At the core of our heart there is always a certain sadness, 'a weeping of the heart,' not because we are sick or morbid, as many claim, but because we are permeated with a strong longing for an ultimate good, and feel continually hampered by daily affairs.

INCLINATION TO PASSIVITY

We have a passive temperament. We are, therefore, not the vivacious, quick, progressive, active propensity of the Fiery or Airy, but are slow, pensive, and reflective. It is difficult to move us to quick action since we have a marked inclination to passivity and inactivity. Our pensive propensity accounts for our fear of suffering and difficulties as well as for our dread of interior exertion and self-denial.

OUR PRIDE HAS ITS VERY PECULIAR SIDE

We do not seek honor or recognition. On the contrary, we are reluctant to appear in public and to be praised. But we are very much afraid of disgrace and humiliation. We often display great reserve and thereby give the impression of modesty and humility. In reality, we retire only because we are afraid of being put to shame. We allow others to be preferred to us, even if they are less qualified and capable than we are for the particular work, position, or office, but at the same time we feel slighted because we are being ignored and our talents are not appreciated. We need to pay very close attention to these feelings of resentment and excessive sensitiveness in the face of even small humiliations.

From what has been said so far, it is evident that it is difficult to deal with us. Because of our peculiarities we are frequently misjudged and treated wrongly. We feel keenly and, therefore, retire and seclude ourselves. Also, we have few friends, because few understand us and because we take few into our confidence.

SEEK JUSTICE

We are vehemently exasperated and provoked by disorder or injustice. The cause of our exasperation is often justifiable, but rarely to the degree felt.

We find peculiar difficulties in correcting people. As said above, we are vehemently excited at the slightest disorder or injustice and feel obliged to correct such disorders, but at the same time we have very little skill or courage in making corrections. We deliberate long on how to express the correction; but when we are about to make it, the words fail us, or we go about it so carefully, so tenderly and reluctantly that it can hardly be called a correction.

The Dark Side of the Earthy Temperament

Reserved

We find it difficult to form new acquaintances and speak little among strangers. We reveal our inmost thoughts reluctantly and only to those whom we trust. We do not easily find the right word to express and describe our sentiments. We yearn often to express our self, because it affords us real relief, to confide the sad, depressing thoughts that burden our heart to a person who sympathizes with us. On the other hand, it requires great exertion on our part to manifest our self, and, when we do so, we go about it so awkwardly that we do not feel satisfied and find no rest. Such experiences tend to make us more reserved.

If we try to master our timidity, we easily fall into the opposite fault of shouting our correction excitedly, angrily, in unsuited or scolding words, so that again our reproach loses its effect. We are unable to discuss things with others; therefore, we swallow our grief and permit many disorders to creep in, although our conscience recognizes the duty to interfere. As teachers, too, we may commit the fault of keeping silent too long about a fault of our charges and when at last we are forced to speak, we do it in such an unfortunate and harsh manner, that the pupils become discouraged and frightened by such admonitions, instead of being encouraged and directed.

Irresolute

On account of too many considerations and too much fear of difficulties and of the possibility that our plans or works may fail, we can hardly reach a decision. We are inclined to defer our decision. What we could do today we postpone for tomorrow, the day after tomorrow, or even for the next week. Then we forget about it and, thus, it happens that what we could have done in an hour takes weeks and months. We are never finished. For many of us it may take a long time to decide about our vocation. We may be a person of missed opportunities. While we see that others have crossed the creek long ago, we still deliberate whether we too should and can jump over it. Because we discover many ways by our reflection and have difficulties in deciding which one to take, we easily give way to others, and do not stubbornly insist on our own opinion.

DESPONDENT

We are timid if we are called upon to begin a new work, to execute a disagreeable task, to venture on a new undertaking. We have a strong will coupled with talent and power, but no courage. It has become proverbial therefore: "Throw the Earthy into the water and he will learn to swim." If we encounter difficulties in our undertakings, even if they are only very insignificant, we feel discouraged and are tempted to give up the ship instead of conquering the obstacle and repairing the ill success by increased effort. We easily lose confidence in others because of slight defects, which we discover in them, or on account of corrections in small matters.

SLOW

We are slow in our thinking. We feel it necessary, first of all, to consider and reconsider everything until we can form a calm and safe judgment. We are also slow in our speech. If we are called upon to answer quickly or to speak without preparation, or if we fear that too much depends on our answer, we become restless and do not find the right word, and consequently often make a false and unsatisfactory reply. Our slow thinking may be the reason why we often stutter, leave our sentences incomplete, use wrong phrases, or search for the right expression. We are also slow, not lazy, at our work. We work carefully and reliably, but only if we have ample time and are not pressed. We naturally do not believe that we are a slow worker.

HOLDS GRUDGES

We can hardly forgive offenses. The first offense we ignore quite easily. But renewed offenses penetrate deeply into our soul and can hardly be forgotten. Strong aversion easily takes root in our heart against persons from whom we have suffered, or in whom we find our fault. Our aversion becomes so strong that we can hardly see these persons without new excitement. We do not want to speak to them and are exasperated by the very thought of them. Usually our aversion is abandoned only after we are separated from persons who incurred our displeasure and at times only after months or even years.

UNTRUSTING

We are very suspicious. We rarely trust people and are always afraid that others have a grudge against us. Thus we often and without cause entertain unjust suspicion about our neighbor, conjecture evil intentions, and fear dangers that do not exist at all.

PESSIMISTIC

We may give way to sad moods, fall into many faults and become a real burden to others. We see everything from the dark side. We are peevish, always drawing attention to the serious side of affairs, complaining regularly about the perversion of people, bad times, downfall of morals, etc. Our motto is: things grow worse all along. Offenses, mishaps, obstacles we always consider much worse than they really are. The consequence is often excessive sadness, unfounded vexation about others, brooding for weeks and weeks on account of real or imaginary insults. We may give way to our disposition to look at everything through a dark glass, gradually become pessimists, that is, persons who always expect a bad result; hypochondriacs, that is, persons who complain continually of insignificant ailments and constantly fear grave sickness; misanthropes, that is, persons who suffer from fear and hatred of others.

THE BRIGHT SIDE OF THE EARTHY TEMPERAMENT

SYMPATHETIC TO PLIGHT OF OTHERS

We are often a great benefactor to others. We have great sympathy others and a keen desire to help them. With an Earthy temperament, we are weak as regards reaction to stimulus, and it is difficult to arouse us. However, after repeated impressions, the reaction is strong and lasting so that we do not forget easily.

Reflective

As regards good qualities that serve as predispositions to virtue, we are inclined to reflection. We are compassionate toward those who suffer, and able to endure suffering to the point of heroism in the performance of our duties. We have a sharp and profound intellect and, because of our natural bent to solitude and reflection, we generally consider matters thoroughly. We may become detached and dry intellectuals or contemplatives. We tend to appreciate the fine arts, but are more drawn to the speculative sciences.

Passionate

When we love, it is with difficulty that we detach ourselves from the object of our love. We suffer greatly if others treat us with coldness or ingratitude. The power of our will is greatly affected by our physical strength and health. If our physical powers are exhausted, our will is weak, but if we are in good health and spirits, we are energetic workers. Normally we do not experience the vehement passions that may torment persons of an Airy temperament. We may say in general that this temperament is opposed to the Airy temperament as the Fiery temperament is opposed to the Watery temperament.

Methods of Self-Training
for the Earthy Temperament

- We should always, especially during attacks of melancholy, say to ourselves: "It is not so bad as I imagine. I see things too darkly," or "I am a pessimist."
- We must from the very beginning resist every feeling of aversion, diffidence, discouragement, or despondency, so that these evil impressions can take no root in our soul.
- We must keep ourselves continually occupied, so that we find no time for brooding. Persevering work will master all.
- We are bound to cultivate the good side of our temperament and especially our inclination to interior life and our sympathy for the suffering of others. We must struggle continually against our weaknesses.
- We can get into bad humor and discouragement on account of the most

insignificant things. If we feel very downcast, we should ask ourselves whether we concerned ourselves too much about the faults of others. Let other people have their own way! Or whether perhaps things do not go according to our own will.

Special Considerations in Balancing the Earthy Temperament

Others should have a sympathetic understanding of we Earthy types. In our entire deportment, we present many riddles to those who do not understand the peculiarities of this temperament type. It is necessary, therefore, to study it and at the same time to find out how our temperament manifests itself. Without this knowledge, great mistakes cannot be avoided.

It is necessary for others to gain our confidence. It is not at all easy and can be done only by giving us a good example in everything and by manifesting an unselfish and sincere love for us. Like an unfolding bud opens to the sun, so the heart of we Earthy persons opens to the sunshine of kindness and love.

Others must always encourage us. Rude reproach, harsh treatment, hardness of heart cast them down and paralyzes our efforts. Friendly advice and patience with their slow actions give us courage and vigor. We will show others gratitude for such kindness.

It is well to keep ourselves always busy, but not to overburden us with work. Because we take everything to heart and are very sensitive, we are in great danger of weakening our nerves. It is necessary, therefore, for us to watch our nervous troubles. Those of us who suffer a nervous breakdown are in a very bad state and cannot recover very easily.

In the training of Earthy children:

- Special care must be taken to be always kind and friendly.
- Encourage and keep them busy.
- Moreover, they must be taught always to pronounce words properly and to use their five senses.
- Special care must be observed in the punishment of Earthy children, otherwise obstinacy and excessive reserve may result.
- Necessary punishment must be given with precaution and great kindness and the slightest appearance of injustice must be carefully avoided.

ACTIONS BASED ON THE
SEVEN NATURE-GIVEN ESSENTIALS

THE ELEMENTS

As Earthy-tempered, we are associated with the Signs: Taurus, Virgo and Capricorn. Earth also symbolizes the natural second, sixth and tenth houses in astrology. We exemplify the matter that everything in the universe is made of. The Earth can be touched and felt as well as seen and heard. Earth is the easiest of the elemental qualities to touch and hold. It is fixed and stable. Earth is the most dense and heaviest of the four elements. Its characteristics are solidity in form, heaviness, being set, that which manifests. In our body it is related to the solid parts like the organs and bones.

In terms of our thoughts:

Earth is associated with thoughts that have crystallized or taken shape. They are the thoughts that are fulfilled or kept as 'solid' attitudes upon which to rely (whether right or not) and upon which action and point of view are built. In action, it is the actual manner in which we do something and what we do.

In feeling, it is not being flexible, but rather being fixed or set. It is the densest part, most often associated with the outward world and the relationship of the body to it.

In mind it relates to those things, which are a 'solid' structure of form that then crystallizes as an echo in the world. Spiritually it is the connection to all matter and the visible form as part of the one body. It is also the densest part of completion of the cycle of manifestation on that corresponding plane. It is heavy. The breath is heavy.[22]

THE HUMOURS

As Earthy types, we tend to be dominated by black bile (atrabilious, melancholic, cold and dry) humour. Even those of us who are balanced may tend to have episodes of the blues. If it continues, we may develop depression. We tend to have a lack of appetite and generally withdraw from society being the introverts that we are. At the same time, our black bile humour helps us 'keep our feet on the ground' and be compassionate towards others.[23]

PHYSIOLOGY

If we are Earthy-tempered, our nervous and emotional system is constantly being challenged with our moodiness, depression and anxiety, all of which increase our Innate Heat. In addition to stomach problems, we may develop nutritional imbalances such as dehydration and anemia.

The Earthy temperament has been described as: "consisting of a cool and thick earthly aspect which is prone to coagulation and a more fluid, vaporous substance. In normal quantities, it stimulates memory and creates a homely, practical, pragmatic, and studious nature. However, its coldest part is adherent and, if not eliminated properly, it can settle on or in tissues and form tumors. The spleen, its receptacle, removes the melancholic element from the blood and body fluids. Signs of excess melancholy element are: fearfulness without a cause; a fearful and foolish imagination; leanness; want of sleep; frightful dreams; sourness in the throat; weak pulse. Melancholics tend to drag their feet and act as if their bodies were a burden to them. They often experience major physical pain from even the most minor injuries."[24]

THE TEMPERAMENT

As people with an Earthy temperament, we seek out that which is attainable, down to earth and not "airy fairy", or "high in the sky". Similar to the element of Earth, we are fixed, organized and predictable as well as being disciplined, stable and dependable. Like the earth, we can only rise so high and even if we were to be on a mountain, it would just mean that we have father to fall. We are responsible and reliable, practical and hardworking, analytical and stable. When our black bile humour is imbalanced, we tend to become "stubborn, lazy, reserved, critical, fussy, pessimistic and snobbish." We are most interested in what is tangible and concrete.[25]

THE BREATH OF LIFE AND INNATE HEAT AS ENERGY GIVERS

As Earthy types we commune with the Earth trying to channel our energy to the parts of our body where are energy is low. We are revived by feeling the healing power of the earth. As we inhale, we sense ourselves as a part of life and our body as connected to the earth. As we exhale we eliminate the poisons and toxins from our body trying to be in harmony with the world around us.[26]

THE ORGANS

Our temperament corresponds to excessive coldness and dryness in the body with the following signs:

- Lack of agility and stiffness in the body and the joints
- Excess of black bile may cause hallucinations
- Constant flatulence
- Bad blood circulation and development of varicose veins
- Poly arthritis
- Enlargement of the stomach
- Excessive appetite, as a consequence of the swollen stomach
- Colic and in some cases vomiting
- Jaundice
- Thickening and possible dryness of nails

THE DIGESTIVE ASSISTANT DRIVES

We are very picky eaters at meal times. It takes us a great deal of time to decide what we want to order at a restaurant but, once it arrives, we enjoy every bite. Being Earth-tempered, we most often have a sour or nervous stomach along with colic, gas, distension and bloating. If we develop an imbalanced temperament, we will harm our digestive process that will lead to chronic stomachaches and stomach problems. Our meal taking needs to be a happy time free from worry and stress including being a fussy eater. At times we may crave sweets and starches to give us a quick boost of energy. Instead we should try to eat a high fiber diet. The appetite of this temperament is variable to poor.[27]

HOW TO MANAGE OUR EARTHY TEMPERAMENT

- Confirm the person even when not asked to do so.
- Give them an opportunity for solitude and reflection.
- Offer support.
- Strive for order and fairness.
- Be accepting of the melancholic as a person and not just their ideas and views.[28]

OVERVIEW

Temperamental quality of Earth.
Overall dominant qualities of **COLDNESS & DRYNESS**.
Any change in the ideal level of coldness and dryness,
especially an increase in these qualities will negatively
affect you.

PERSONALITY:	INCREASE IN COLD & DRYNESS CAN BE A RESULT OF:

PERSONALITY:

- Organized
- Reliable
- Ambitious
- Thoughtful
- Humanitarian
- Well-Liked
- Reserved
- Indecisive
- Rigid
- Critical

INCREASE IN COLD & DRYNESS CAN BE A RESULT OF:

- Cold and Dry Tempered Foods
- Rainy Season
- Cold and Moist Environment
- Sadness and Anxiety
- Lack of Exercise
- Excessive Rest and Sleep
- Early Winter

APPETITE Varies and fluctuates depending on mental/nervous/emotional state.

DIGESTION Typically irregular to poor digestion, which varies according to mental/ nervous/emotional state. Gas and bloating is common with this Temperament.

6 NURTURE-GIVEN ESSENTIALS FOR EARTH PRIMARY

AIR & ENVIRONMENT	Any activity and environment that increase coldness and dryness will negatively affect you. Seashore and coastal areas are beneficial for your health.
PHYSICAL REST & ACTIVITY	Moderate and light exercise for a short duration is best. Walking for 15 minutes after dinner is also beneficial.
SLEEP & WAKEFULNESS	Getting to bed early and sleeping for 6-8 hours is best. These individuals are more prone to insomnia. Avoid staying up too late as this will have a negative affect on your temperament.
EMOTIONS & AROMATHERAPY	Try to avoid feelings of loneliness, depression and grief. These qualities will have a negative influence on this temperament, especially if prolonged or excessive.
RETENTION & EVACUATION	Prevent over drying your body by applying moisturizers on your skin. Drink three liters of water per day. Bodily wastes should never be held in or forced to leave.
FOOD, DIET & DRINK	Eat mostly hot and wet foods and occasionally hot and dry foods. Eat less cold and wet foods and the least amount of cold and dry foods.

WHAT TO EAT

Melancholic
Earth
Cold & Dry

MEATS & FISH

WET VEGGIES

WET FRUITS

SPICES & HERBS

FLOUR & GRAINS

NUTS & SEEDS

COOKING OILS

Visit avicennacuisine.com for a full database of ingredients.

CHAPTER 21

Watery TEMPERAMENT
Humour: Phlegm
Basic Qualities: Cold and Wet

The Characteristics of the Watery Temperament

Our soul or mind is only weakly or not at all touched by impressions. The reaction is feeble or entirely missing. Eventual impressions fade away very soon.

The Watery Temperament:

1 We are slow paced and stubborn.
2 We are slow in making decisions.
3 We are indifferent to external affairs.
4 We are perhaps overcautious in minor matters.
5 We are reserved and distant.
6 We expend as little energy as possible for a task.
7 We have a marked tendency to persevere.
8 We tend to have constancy of mood.

The Fundamental Disposition of the Watery Temperament

Uninterested in the World Around Us

We have little interest in what goes on around us. While we often speak of the great thoughts that we have, the amazing books we could write, the world class paintings that we could paint, we never do these things because it would require too much energy. We tend to live by and for ourselves, almost to the point of egoism.

SLOW PACED

We may also have little inclination to work, preferring leisure instead. With us, everything develops slowly. It is not clear if we really have low energy or if we just refuse to use the energy that we have. It is our slowness and calmness that causes us to lose many good opportunities because we delay so long in putting works into operation.

TASK ORIENTED

While we have a great capacity for work and especially for work that requires precision and accuracy, we put only a minimal amount of energy into the task at hand.

PEACE LOVING

We are naturally suited to be negotiators and diplomats.

CALM AND EASYGOING

We do not fear rejection by others and are unconcerned by people's hostile reactions to us. We are calm and easygoing and rarely suffer from exaggerated feelings or emotional outbursts except when we are at a low energy level.

OBSERVER

We tend to sit back and observe situations not getting involved because it would require too much energy expenditure on our part. In doing so, we are often judgmental and sarcastic in regard to others.

THE DARK SIDE OF THE WATERY TEMPERAMENT

STUBBORN AND IRON WILLED

As Watery-tempered individuals, we are very stubborn when it comes to making changes. Even Fiery-tempered persons are not able to control us which causes great frustration to them.

FRUSTRATE THOSE WHO LOVE US

As we are easygoing and seldom harbor bitterness towards others, our cool and complacent attitude tends to hurt those who love us. We rarely give of ourselves and, as a result, we rarely receive from others.

VERBAL ABUSER

When we do have an occasional outburst of anger, we can be very hurtful through the verbal abuse that we place on another person. Our verbal abuse is to protect our low level of energy in terms of either physical or sexual involvement.

INDECISIVE

Our indecisiveness causes us to avoid becoming involved in any deep relationships. We prefer just to observe. Being indecisive and resisting change, we tend to stay uninvolved and dampen the enthusiasm of those around us.

TENDENCY TO PROCRASTINATE

In our procrastinating, we are unemotional in inexpressive, rarely sacrificing our own time and efforts for others. We tend to be lazy and careless discouraging others we may work with.

DIFFICULT TO MOTIVATE

We often harbor negative emotions that can dominate our temperament. We become fearful, addicted to worrying, selfish, avoid responsibility, shy and self-righteous, that is, having a strong belief that our own opinions, etc. are right and the other people's are wrong. We, then, become intolerant of the opinions and behaviors of others that do not agree with our sense of righteousness. At times we lack self-motivation and any goals we may have set for ourselves. We do not want to be pushed.

Moody

When we are under stress, we tend to become moody, fearful and sentimental. Our moods are changeable and come and go in waves and tides, one minute happy and the next sad.

The Bright Side of the Watery Temperament

Detail Oriented

Our good characteristics are that we work slowly but assiduously. We are able to perform tasks that appear to be tedious to others as we work very efficiently and are perfectionists in our work but not when it comes to our home where we are often very disorganized. We are prudent, sensible, reflective, and work with a measured pace. We attain our goals without fanfare or violence because we usually avoid difficulties rather than attacking them.

Work Well in a Hostile Setting

As we are calm and easygoing, we are able to work well in a hostile setting without becoming emotionally involved. We are most often relaxed, consistent and kind towards others, sympathetic and kindhearted.

Stable

As the Watery type, we are the most stable of the temperaments. We tend to make friends easily in a short period of time as we are a good listener, show concern, compassion and, when required, a sense of humour. Our low-key personality results in our being stable as long as we let go of our selfishness and self-righteous attitude. We are not easily irritated by insults, misfortunes, or sickness. We usually remain tranquil, discreet, and sober. We have a great deal of common sense and mental balance.

Identify Injustice

We are good at identifying injustice wherever we find it, but we seldom, if ever, take any action against it. Instead we try to inspire others to get involved.

PRACTICAL

We tend to be conservative and practical as well as being peace loving, well balanced and patient. We have good hearts, but we seem to be cold. We would sacrifice to the point of heroism if it was necessary, but we lack enthusiasm and spontaneity because we are reserved and somewhat lazy by nature.

SENSITIVE

We have the ability to exhibit deep feelings. We are sympathetic and empathetic and have a wonderful sense of imagination resulting in many of us being artistic as well as romantic. We prefer safe and comfortable situations.

GENTLE

We are gentle, sweet and mild almost timid at times and are disposed to try to please everyone. We make strong emotional connections with the ones that we love and suffer a great deal if a relationship does not work out. We do not possess the inflammable passions of the Airy temperament, the deep passions of the Earthy temperament, or the ardent passions of the Fiery temperament.

REALISTIC

We are realistic in our demands for affection and love. In our speech we are orderly, clear, positive, and measured, rather than florid and picturesque. We are more suited to scientific work that involves long and patient research and minute investigation than to original productions.

METHODS OF SELF-TRAINING
FOR THE WATERY TEMPERAMENT

- We need to get more sleep as this is the best way we have to renew our energy.
- We need a great deal of encouragement and praise
- We need to be treated very nicely.

- We need to avoid too much exposure to over stimulating environments
- We can avoid the bad effects of our temperament if we are inculcated with deep convictions
- With deep convictions, we demand of ourselves methodical and constant efforts toward greater perfection.
- We will advance slowly, but we will advance far.
- We must not be allowed to become inactive and apathetic
- We need to direct ourselves to some lofty ideal. We, too, need to gain control of ourselves, not as the Fiery, who must restrain and moderate themselves, but to arouse ourselves and put their dormant powers to good use.

SPECIAL CONSIDERATIONS IN BALANCING THE WATERY TEMPERAMENT

As Watery-tempered individuals, we have a very fragile ego that we never let on about. When forced to make a decision out of some necessity and blamed when it does not work out, this is detrimental to our self-esteem.

We feel that people take advantage of our easygoing temperament so that we become an easy target for someone to misuse us.

When our first reaction to something is "no," others should continue to show us confidence saying that we do have the ability to lead or make sound decisions.

We need time and some space to adjust to changes and it is easier for us to do so if we are given sufficient information and encouragement.

We need constant show of appreciation by others for our kind and even temperament as we suffer deeply from a sense of abandonment. We sense this when we feel we are not appreciated. We are easily hurt.

We do not work well when we are forced to do things in a hurry.

In educating Watery-tempered children:

- They need direct and positive motivation.
- Do not expect them to respond in immediate enthusiasm. It is not part of their nature.
- Instead of pushing or judging, help them set goals and provide them with benchmark rewards.
- Training of Watery-tempered children is very difficult, because external

influence has little effect upon them and internal personal motives are lacking.

- It is necessary to explain everything most minutely to them and repeat it again and again, so that at least some impression may be made to last and to accustom them by patience and charity to follow strictly a well-planned rule of life.
- The application of corporal punishment is less dangerous in the education of Watery children. It is much more beneficial to them than to other children, especially to those of Fiery or Earthy temperament.

ACTIONS BASED ON THE
SEVEN NATURE-GIVEN ESSENTIALS

THE ELEMENTS

As among the Watery-tempered, we are associated with the Signs Cancer, Scorpio and Pisces. The element of Water also represents the natural fourth, eighth and twelfth houses in astrology.

Water rises into the air and falls as rain, nurturing the land. The earth absorbs it to become fertile. We can go for weeks without food, but only days without water. Living things need water. With it they grow and mature. Without it they die. Normally water is cold, that is, it absorbs energy. It takes in the energy of others. Water is more sensitive than the other elements in that it can appear in the three forms of matter: solid like the earth; liquid—its normal state—and as vapor—like air. Water, like earth, is heavy, and falls to the earth. It is less easily constrained than earth, but more easily than fire or air. Yet water can rise up into the air (although it often falls again as rain.) Unlike fire and air it forms a flat surface, therefore, like earth, it has some form. Air is less limited than the earth, but more limited than fire and air. While fire cannot be contained, it disappears if you totally enclose it, and air expands to fill any container. Water is more limited and keeps it volume, and has a level. While fire cannot destroy the earth, water can. It is the universal solvent that has the potential to make everyone one, without destroying that which it unites. Water can rise high with the help of air, but generally does not move upwards. Water is extremely powerful, and will always find its own level. If artificially constrained at a high level, it will eventually break free, but then it will fall. Water is impressionable and reflective. It can go deep. Archetypal water refers to the feelings and the emotions. It refers to the unconscious mind.[29]

The Humours

Having a dominant phlegmatic humour, we tend to be slow and lacking in drive. This, however, means that we are calm and stable. With these abilities, we are able to concentrate for long periods of time and reach the best conclusions for the various situations with which we are faced.[30]

Physiology

In terms of physiology as a Watery-tempered person, our body's function is to eliminate unnecessary matter from our body.

Phlegm plays a necessary role in the body during short periods of intense activity in the body such as the cold and flu; however, copious amounts of phlegm are expelled by the body through the nose in an attempt to clear out toxins and bacteria. The phlegmatic humour has a beneficial cooling and moistening effect on the heart, and strengthens the function of the lower brain and the emotions. Phlegm maintains proper fat metabolism and the balance of body fluids, electrolytes, and hormones through the circulation of lymph and moisture through the body in the same manner that sanguine, or blood, provides nutrition through the circulation system. Its receptacle is the lungs. Signs of excess phlegm in the system can be exhibited by sleepiness; dullness; slowness; heaviness; cowardliness; forgetfulness; frequent spitting; runny nose; little appetite for meat; bad digestion; and white and cold skin. Many practitioners have observed that phlegmatic types often possess many of the following qualities: pale, smooth, soft, cold and moist skin; dark blond or blond hair; hairless bodies; shortness of stature; flabby and fat body build; poor appetites; slow or weak digestion; thin and pale urine; pale and loose feces; dreams of water; and apathy.[31]

The Temperament

As the Watery type, we speak to feelings, imagination and creative experiences. We tend to be sensitive, sympathetic, intuitive, domestic, artistic and receptive. When we are suffering from an imbalance of phlegmatic humour, our negative traits make us moody, brooding, unrealistic and secretive.[32]

THE BREATH OF LIFE AND INNATE HEAT AS ENERGY GIVERS

The Breath of a Watery-tempered person develops a sense of flow and vitality that helps bring about a sense of creativity. This allows those of us who are of the Watery type to break from any habitual thinking patterns that we have developed. We feel energized and a sense of renewal when we inhale and exhale.[33]

THE ORGANS

As the Watery type we often complain of soreness and pain in our lumbar region; thinning and loss of head hair; weakness and pain in our ankles, knees and hips; weakness in hearing and vision; impotence; infertility and possibly genetic impairments. We may suffer from disorders of the central nervous system; diseases of the spinal column, bones, teeth and joints; and disorders in our fluid metabolism.[34]

THE DIGESTIVE ASSISTANT DRIVES

We are usually the last one to finish a meal. This leads to our gaining weight because we remain too long at the table or lose weight because we just pick at our food or because we chew it too well. We can attain a balance by "keeping away from phlegm-inducing foods such as Milk, Wheat and Sweets, eating more heating foods, and engaging in more heating activities. We benefit from the herbs Anise, Cinnamon, Valerian Root, Fenugreek, Cardamom, Garlic, and Ginger."[35]

HOW TO MANAGE THE WATERY TEMPERAMENT

- Openly affirm and acknowledge the Watery-tempered person.
- Give the person time for relaxation.
- Praise them when they take a leadership role. Help them to increase their confidence to accepting challenges.
- Use gentle reminders, but do not criticize or take over.
- Be specific when making requests and state them positively.[36]

OVERVIEW

Temperamental quality of Water.
Overall dominant qualities of **COLDNESS & WETNESS.**
Any change in the ideal level of coldness and wetness especially an increase in these qualities will negatively affect you.

PERSONALITY:

- Creative
- Imaginative
- Artistic
- Intuitive
- Easy-Going
- Trustworthy
- Moody
- Vulnerable
- Secretive
- Compulsive

INCREASE IN COLD & WETNESS CAN BE A RESULT OF:

- Cold and Wet Tempered Foods
- Rainy Season
- Cold and Humid Environment
- Sadness and Anxiety
- Lack of Exercise
- Excessive Rest and Sleep
- Early Winter

APPETITE Tends to be slow but steady with cravings for sweets, dairy products, and starchy foods.

DIGESTION Slow but steady digestion. These individuals tend to feel tired and sluggish after meals.

6 NURTURE-GIVEN ESSENTIALS FOR WATER PRIMARY

AIR & ENVIRONMENT	Cold air negatively affects a dominant Watery temperament. Cold and wet environments and air conditioners should be avoided as much as possible.
PHYSICAL REST & ACTIVITY	Exercising on a daily basis will have a positive affect on you. Vigorous exercise for a longer duration is beneficial. Avoid unnecessary rest during the daytime. Stay active.
SLEEP & WAKEFULNESS	This temperament requires a good nights sleep of 6-7 hours. More than this can be harmful. These individuals should get up early in the morning and avoid napping during the day.
EMOTIONS & AROMATHERAPY	Be aware and manage your emotions. This temperament tends to have fear, shyness and depression.
RETENTION & EVACUATION	Sweating is healthy for this temperament and laxatives are also beneficial. An imbalance in this temperament will create phlegm congestion and slow digestion.
FOOD, DIET & DRINK	Eat mostly hot and dry foods and occasionally cold and dry foods. Eat less hot and wet foods and the least amount of cold and wet foods.

WHAT TO EAT

Phlegmatic
Water
Cold & Wet

MEATS & FISH

DRY VEGGIES

DRY FRUITS

SPICES & HERBS

FLOUR & GRAINS

NUTS & SEEDS

COOKING OILS

Visit avicennacuisine.com for a full database of ingredients.

CHAPTER 22

Mixed Temperaments: Primary/Secondary

A PERSON CAN HAVE A SO-CALLED MIXED TEMPERAMENT. Mixed Temperaments are those in which one Temperament predominates while another Temperament also manifests itself. It will be a great help in such cases to know the Temperaments of the parents of such person. If father and mother are of the same Temperament, the children will probably inherit the Temperament of the parents. If father and mother are of a fiery (hot and dry) Temperament, the children will also be fiery (hot and dry). If, however, the father and mother are of different Temperaments, the children will inherit the different Temperaments. If, for instance, the father is of a fiery (hot and dry) Temperament and the mother earthy (cold and dry), the children will be either fiery (hot and dry) with a earthy (cold and dry) mixture, or earthy (cold and dry) with a fiery (hot and dry) tendency, according to the degree of influence of either of the two parents. In order to learn the predominant Temperament, it is absolutely necessary to follow closely the above-mentioned questions concerning the Temperaments. But it also happens, although not so often as many believe, that in one person two Temperaments are so mixed that both are equally strong.

If, for instance, you have a fiery primary temperament and airy secondary temperament, this means you have a primary hot and dry temperament and secondary hot and wet. Your temperament will be somewhere between hot and dry and hot and wet. Heat is the common quality. Your ideal state has a dominate quality of heat, then dryness and then moisture.

Any change in this ideal temperament for you will have a negative effect upon your health. As heat is the dominant quality, changes in the level of heat (excess of heat) will affect you more than any other qualities. Any changes in the quality of moistness will have the least negative effect.

AIR AND FIRE

The Airy-Fiery temperament is similar to the Fiery-Airy temperament; only the Airy characteristics prevail, the Fiery ones recede to the background. Excitement and reaction are quick and vehement and the impression does not fade so quickly as with the pure Airy, even though it does not penetrate so far as with the pure Fiery.

PRIMARY   SECONDARY

OVERVIEW

Temperamental quality between Air and Fire.
Overall dominant quality of **HEAT**.
Any change in the ideal level of heat, especially an
increase in heat will negatively affect you.

PERSONALITY:

- Strong Extrovert
- People-Oriented
- Enthusiastic
- Resolute
- Productive
- Sports Enthusiast
- Ideal in Sales
- Forgetful
- Stubborn
- Justifies Actions

INCREASE IN HEAT CAN BE A RESULT OF:

- Hot and Wet and Hot and Dry Tempered Foods
- Very Hot Weather
- Summer Heat and Humidity
- Excessive Anger
- Lack of Sleep
- Vigorous Exercise

APPETITE   The epicure. A craving for rich gourmet foods. Typically quite hearty. Can also be fond of fried, spicy and salty foods with intense taste sensations.

DIGESTION   Good to moderate digestion, but can be overwhelmed by excessive food. These individuals can also tend to easily digest a wide variety of foods.

6 NURTURE-GIVEN ESSENTIALS FOR AIR PRIMARY & FIRE SECONDARY

AIR & ENVIRONMENT	Fresh air and a cool, properly ventilated environment are most ideal.
PHYSICAL REST & ACTIVITY	Exercise in the early morning and late afternoon. Avoid excessive movement.
SLEEP & WAKEFULNESS	This temperament requires a good nights sleep of 6-8 hours.
EMOTIONS & AROMATHERAPY	Avoid extreme emotions of anger, excitability, and irritability as much as possible. This can be managed with breathing exercises and meditation.
RETENTION & EVACUATION	Drink plenty of water to avoid and eliminate excess heat and dryness. Laxatives are also beneficial.
FOOD, DIET & DRINK	Eat mostly cold and dry foods and occasionally cold and wet foods. Eat less hot and dry foods and the least amount of hot and wet foods.

AIR AND WATER

The Airy-Watery temperament is overwhelmed with the Airy dominant and the Watery subordinate. People with these temperaments are carefree and happy to spend their lives trying to help others. They would not intend to hurt others, but may lack motivation for a workplace. They prefer visiting and social life to work.

PRIMARY   **SECONDARY**

OVERVIEW

Temperamental quality between Air and Water.
Overall dominant quality of **WETNESS**.
Any change in the ideal level of wetness, especially an increase in wetness will negatively affect you.

PERSONALITY:

- Gracious
- Easygoing
- Carefree
- Happy
- Help Others
- Overpowering
- Outgoing
- Lacks Motivation
- Lacks Discipline

INCREASE IN WETNESS CAN BE A RESULT OF:

- Hot and Wet and Cold and Wet Tempered Foods
- Rainy Season
- Wet and Humid Environment
- Lack of Exercise
- Sadness and Anxiety

APPETITE   The epicure. A craving for rich gourmet foods. Typically quite hearty. Can also tend to have a slow appetite with cravings for sweets, dairy products and starchy foods.

DIGESTION   Good to moderate digestion, but can be overwhelmed by excessive food. These individuals can also tend to feel tired and sluggish after meals.

6 NURTURE-GIVEN ESSENTIALS FOR AIR PRIMARY & WATER SECONDARY

AIR & ENVIRONMENT	Avoid staying in hot and moist air for a long period of time. These individuals can tolerate cold easily.
PHYSICAL REST & ACTIVITY	Avoid inadequate rest and vigorous activity. Light training and aerobics for 15-20 minutes suit you best.
SLEEP & WAKEFULNESS	This temperament requires a good nights sleep of 6-7 hours. Going to bed early is best for the dominant Airy temperament.
EMOTIONS & AROMATHERAPY	Excessive excitement, worry, anger or emotional excess should be avoided. Deep breathing exercises are beneficial.
RETENTION & EVACUATION	A high fiber diet is best for this temperament in order to maintain regular bowel habits. Drink plenty of water. Laxatives are also recommended.
FOOD, DIET & DRINK	Eat mostly cold and dry foods and occasionally hot and dry foods. Eat less cold and wet foods and the least amount of hot and wet foods.

FIRE AND EARTH

Here, two serious, passionate temperaments are mixed; the pride, obstinacy, and anger of the Fiery with the morose, unsocial, reserved temper of the Earthy. Persons who have such a mixture of temperaments must cultivate a great deal of self-control, in order to acquire interior peace and not to become a burden to those with whom they work and live.

PRIMARY   SECONDARY

OVERVIEW

Temperamental quality between Fire and Earth.
Overall dominant quality of **DRYNESS**.
Any change in the ideal level of dryness, especially an increase in dryness will negatively affect you.

PERSONALITY:

- Industrious
- Capable
- Goal-Oriented
- Detailed
- Attentive
- Competitive
- Forceful
- Sarcastic
- Hostile
- Perfectionist

INCREASE IN DRYNESS CAN BE A RESULT OF:

- Hot and Dry and Cold and Dry Tempered Foods
- Hot Weather
- Summer Heat
- Excessive Anger
- Lack of Sleep
- Irregular Bowel Movements
- Vigorous Exercise

APPETITE Carnivore, enjoys fried, salty or spicy foods. Craves intense or stimulating taste sensations, but can vary according to mental/nervous/emotional state.

DIGESTION Able to digest everything quickly when balanced and healthy. There's a tendency to have irregular digestion depending on mental, nervous, and emotional state.

6 NURTURE–GIVEN ESSENTIALS FOR FIRE PRIMARY & EARTH SECONDARY

AIR & ENVIRONMENT	Fresh air and a cool, properly ventilated environment are most ideal.
PHYSICAL REST & ACTIVITY	Exercise in the early morning and late afternoon. Avoid excessive movement.
SLEEP & WAKEFULNESS	This temperament requires a good nights sleep of 6-8 hours.
EMOTIONS & AROMATHERAPY	Avoid extreme emotions of anger, excitability, and irritability as much as possible. This can be managed with breathing exercises and meditation.
RETENTION & EVACUATION	Drink plenty of water to avoid and eliminate excess heat and dryness. Laxatives are also beneficial.
FOOD, DIET & DRINK	Eat mainly cold and wet foods and occasionally hot and wet foods. Eat less cold and dry foods and the least amount of hot and dry foods.

FIRE AND AIR

In the Fiery-Airy temperament the excitement is quick, and the re-action also; but the impression is not so lasting as with the pure Fiery temperament. The pride of the Fiery is mixed with vanity; the anger and obstinacy are not so strong, but more moderate than in the pure choleric. This is a very happy combination.

OVERVIEW

Temperamental quality between Fire and Air.
Overall dominant quality of **HEAT.**
Any change in the ideal level of heat, especially an
increase in heat will negatively affect you.

PERSONALITY:

- Extrovert
- Active
- Purposeful
- Fearless
- Energetic
- Engaged
- Quick to Anger
- Resentment
- Impatient
- Opinionated

INCREASE IN HEAT CAN BE A RESULT OF:

- Hot and Dry and Hot and Wet Tempered Foods
- Very Hot Weather
- Summer Heat
- Excessive Anger
- Lack of Sleep
- Vigorous Exercise

APPETITE Carnivore, enjoys fried, salty or spicy foods. Craves intense or stimulating taste sensations. The epicure.

DIGESTION Able to digest everything quickly when balanced and healthy. If unhealthy, there's a tendency towards gastritis, hyperacidity, and acid reflux. Can be overwhelmed by excessive food.

6 NURTURE-GIVEN ESSENTIALS FOR
FIRE PRIMARY & AIR SECONDARY

AIR & ENVIRONMENT	Fresh air and a cool, properly ventilated environment are most ideal. Avoid very hot climates. In the summer season, keep cool at all times.
PHYSICAL REST & ACTIVITY	Exercise in the early morning and late afternoon. Avoid vigorous exercise and strenuous movements.
SLEEP & WAKEFULNESS	This temperament requires a good nights sleep of 6-8 hours.
EMOTIONS & AROMATHERAPY	Avoid extreme emotions of anger, excitability, and irritability as much as possible. This can be managed with breathing exercises and meditation.
RETENTION & EVACUATION	Drink plenty of water to avoid and eliminate excess heat. Laxatives are also beneficial.
FOOD, DIET & DRINK	Eat mostly cold and wet foods and occasionally cold and dry foods. Eat less hot and wet foods and the least amount of hot and dry foods.

WATER AND AIR

This combination of Watery and Earthy are easy to get along with. They are considered to be people oriented. They may tend towards a lack of discipline and motivation as well.

OVERVIEW

Temperamental quality between Water and Air.
Overall dominant quality of **WETNESS**.
Any change in the ideal level of wetness, especially an increase in wetness will negatively affect you.

PERSONALITY:

- Easy-Going
- Group Leader
- Good Listener
- Practical
- Helpful
- Trustworthy
- Stubborn
- Passive
- Uncooperative
- Unmotivated

INCREASE IN WETNESS CAN BE A RESULT OF:

- Cold and Wet and Hot and Wet Tempered Foods
- Rainy Season
- Cold and Humid Environment
- Sadness and Anxiety
- Lack of Exercise
- Excessive Rest and Sleep
- Early Winter

APPETITE Tends to be slow but steady with cravings for sweets, dairy products, and starchy foods. Can also have an appetite for rich gourmet foods.

DIGESTION Slow but steady digestion. These individuals tend to feel tired and sluggish after meals. Can be overwhelmed by excessive amounts of foods.

6 NURTURE-GIVEN ESSENTIALS FOR WATER PRIMARY & AIR SECONDARY

AIR & ENVIRONMENT	Cold air negatively affects a dominant Watery temperament. Cold and wet environments and air conditioners should be avoided as much as possible.
PHYSICAL REST & ACTIVITY	Exercising on a daily basis will have a positive affect. Avoid unnecessary rest during the daytime. Stay active.
SLEEP & WAKEFULNESS	This temperament requires a good nights sleep of 7-8 hours. More than this can be harmful.
EMOTIONS & AROMATHERAPY	Avoid extreme emotions of anger, excitability, and irritability as much as possible. This can be managed with breathing exercises and meditation.
RETENTION & EVACUATION	Sweating is healthy for this temperament and laxatives are also beneficial. An imbalance in this temperament will create phlegm congestion and slow digestion.
FOOD, DIET & DRINK	Eat mostly hot and dry foods and occasionally cold and dry foods. Eat less hot and wet foods and the least amount of cold and wet foods.

WATER AND EARTH

The Watery-Earthy combination creates a person who is dependable, gracious and quiet. They move between having patience and being critical. They may avoid group activities.

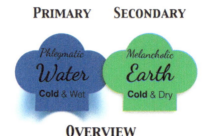

PRIMARY   SECONDARY

Phlegmatic
Water
Cold & Wet

Melancholic
Earth
Cold & Dry

OVERVIEW

Temperamental quality between Water and Earth.
Overall dominant quality of **COLDNESS**.
Any change in the ideal level of coldness, especially an increase in coldness will negatively affect you.

PERSONALITY:

- Organized
- Humanitarian
- Well-Liked
- Scholarly
- Introverted
- Low Energy
- Fearful
- Anxious
- Easily Discouraged
- Perfectionist

INCREASE IN COLDNESS CAN BE A RESULT OF:

- Cold and Wet and Cold and Dry Tempered Foods
- Rainy Season
- Cold Environment
- Sadness and Anxiety
- Lack of Exercise
- Excessive Rest and Sleep
- Early or Late Winter
- Irregular Eating Habits

APPETITE Tends to be slow but steady with cravings for sweets, dairy products, and starchy foods. Also varies according to mental/nervous/emotional state.

DIGESTION Slow but steady digestion. These individuals tend to feel tired and sluggish after meals. Digestion also varies according to mental/nervous/ emotional state.

6 NURTURE-GIVEN ESSENTIALS FOR WATER PRIMARY & EARTH SECONDARY

AIR & ENVIRONMENT	Cold air negatively affects a dominant Watery temperament. Cold environments should be avoided. Dress warm and seek warm environments.
PHYSICAL REST & ACTIVITY	Exercising on a daily basis will have a positive affect. Avoid unnecessary rest during the daytime. Stay active.
SLEEP & WAKEFULNESS	This temperament requires a good nights sleep of 8 hours. Rising before sunrise will help eliminate excess phlegm.
EMOTIONS & AROMATHERAPY	Try to avoid extreme emotions of anger, excitability, shyness and irritability as much as possible. This can be managed with breathing exercises and meditation.
RETENTION & EVACUATION	Sweating is healthy for this temperament and laxatives are also beneficial. An imbalance in this temperament will create phlegm congestion and slow digestion.
FOOD, DIET & DRINK	Eat mostly hot and dry foods and occasionally hot and wet foods. Eat less cold and dry foods and the least amount of cold and wet foods.

EARTH AND FIRE

Both the Earthy and Fiery types are perfectionists. They have both determination and are decisive. They may have the Earthy quality of being hard to please. They may tend to hold grudges. They may tend towards being excessively concerned with or critical of inconsequential details.

PRIMARY   SECONDARY

Melancholic
Earth
Cold & **Dry**

Choleric
Fire
Hot & **Dry**

OVERVIEW

Temperamental quality between Earth and Fire.
Overall dominant quality of **DRYNESS**.
Any change in the ideal level of dryness, especially an increase in dryness will negatively affect you.

PERSONALITY:

- Self-Willed
- Strong Leader
- Perfectionist
- Drives Others
- Decisive
- Determined
- Nit-Picker
- Revengeful
- Snark
- Bitter

INCREASE IN DRYNESS CAN BE A RESULT OF:

- Cold and Dry and Hot and Dry Tempered Foods
- Very Hot Weather
- Anger
- Vigorous Exercise
- Irregular Rest & Sleep Patterns
- Late Winter
- Irregular Elimination and Evacuation

APPETITE Varies and fluctuates depending on mental/nervous/emotional state. Can have a tendency towards eating fried, salty, spicy foods with intense flavors.

DIGESTION Typically irregular to poor digestion, which varies according to mental/nervous/emotional state. Those who have an equally Fiery Temperament have a faster digestion system.

ACTIONS BASED ON THE SIX NURTURING ESSENTIALS

6 NURTURE-GIVEN ESSENTIALS FOR
EARTH PRIMARY & FIRE SECONDARY

AIR & ENVIRONMENT

Any activity and environment that increase coldness and dryness will negatively affect you. Damp weather can also bother this temperament combination.

PHYSICAL REST & ACTIVITY

Moderate and light exercise for a short duration is best. Walking for 15 minutes after dinner is also beneficial.

SLEEP & WAKEFULNESS

Getting to bed early and sleeping for 6-8 hours is best. These individuals are more prone to insomnia. Avoid staying up too late as this will have a negative affect on your temperament.

EMOTIONS & AROMATHERAPY

Try to avoid feelings of loneliness, depression and grief. These qualities will have a negative influence on this temperament, especially if prolonged or excessive.

RETENTION & EVACUATION

Prevent over drying your body by applying moisturizers on your skin. Drink three liters of water per day. Bodily wastes should never be held in or forced to leave.

FOOD, DIET & DRINK

Eat mostly hot and wet foods and occasionally cold and wet foods. Eat less hot and dry foods and the least amount of cold and dry foods.

EARTH AND WATER

People of our type succeed better in community life than the pure Earthy. They lack, more or less, the morose, gloomy, brooding propensity of the Earthy and are happily aided by the quiet apathy of the Watery. Such people do not easily take offense; they can readily bear injuries and are contented and steady laborers.

PRIMARY SECONDARY

OVERVIEW

Temperamental quality between Earth and Water.
Overall dominant quality of **COLDNESS**.
Any change in the ideal level of coldness, especially an increase in coldness will negatively affect you.

PERSONALITY:

- Organized
- Humanitarian
- Well-Liked
- Scholarly
- Introverted
- Low Energy
- Fearful
- Anxious
- Easily Discouraged
- Perfectionist

INCREASE IN COLDNESS CAN BE A RESULT OF:

- Cold and Dry and Cold and Wet Tempered Foods
- Rainy Season
- Cold Environment
- Sadness and Anxiety
- Lack of Exercise
- Excessive Rest and Sleep
- Early or Late Winter
- Irregular Eating Habits

APPETITE Varies and fluctuates depending on mental/nervous/emotional state. Tends to crave more sweets, dairy products and starchy foods.

DIGESTION Irregular to poor digestion, which varies according to mental/nervous/emotional state. Can tend to feel slow and sluggish after meals.

6 Nurture-Given Essentials for Earth Primary & Water Secondary

Air & Environment	Any activity and environment that increases coldness and dryness will negatively affect you. Damp weather can also bother this temperament combination.
Physical Rest & Activity	Moderate and light exercise for a short duration is best. Walking for 15 minutes after dinner is also beneficial.
Sleep & Wakefulness	Getting to bed early and sleeping for 6-8 hours is best. These individuals are more prone to insomnia. Avoid staying up too late as this will have a negative affect on your temperament.
Emotions & Aromatherapy	Try to avoid feelings of loneliness, depression and grief. These qualities will have a negative influence on this temperament, especially if prolonged or excessive.
Retention & Evacuation	Prevent over drying your body by applying moisturizers on your skin. Drink three liters of water per day. Bodily wastes should never be held in or forced to leave.
Food, Diet & Drink	Eat mostly hot and wet foods and occasionally hot and dry foods. Eat less cold and wet foods and the least amount of cold and dry foods.

CHAPTER 23

The Temperament Test

WHAT AVICENNA CUISINE DOES FOR YOU

BY TAKING THE FOLLOWING TEMPERAMENT TEST, you will have determined some aspects of your body-mind-energy Primary and possibly Secondary Temperament. The primary four humours are:

1 **Blood** (sanguine, hot and wet, salty)
2 **Yellow Bile** (choleric, hot and dry, bitter)
3 **Water** (phlegmatic, cold and wet, sweet)
4 **Black Bile** (melancholic, cold and dry, sour)

These humours provide the energy for our Temperament. With Avicenna Cuisine, we refer to the four Temperaments as:

1 **Airy (Hot and Wet)**
2 **Fiery (Hot and Dry)**
3 **Watery (Cold and Wet)**
4 **Earthy (Cold and Dry)**

While Avicenna Cuisine is an integrative system, it is similar in many ways to alternative systems such as Ayurveda, Chinese, Tibetan, Japanese, and so forth, in the sense of maintaining a balance to be able to live a healthy life. A balance is maintained through exhibiting the strengths of your Temperament, determined by whether or not your Temperament is hot or cold (active qualities) or dry or wet (passive qualities).

Of course, there are many factors that enter into determining your Temperament: Place of birth, Temperament of your parents and gender, among others. In addition, your original Temperament may change somewhat over time depending upon your age. The Temperament Test simply gives you a general picture of some of the characteristics of your nature, but is not exhaustive. Temperament is expressed through your humours, the presence of the elemental qualities and the ABC of the self (affect, behavior and cognition).

In the same way that you have a basic, predisposed physical Temperament that shows itself through your emotions, your behavior and the way you think, your strengths are strengthened or weaknesses weakened by the property of the food that you eat. As each of you is an individual, with an individual nature, maintaining a balance of health depends on your eating the right tempered foods for your particular Temperament.

It is very important, and indeed necessary to determine, first of all, your basic Temperament by answering these questions, to be able to refer the various symptoms of the different Temperaments to their proper source. Only then can self-knowledge be deepened to a full realization of how far the various light and dark sides of your Temperament are developed, and of the modifications and variations your predominant Temperament may have undergone by mixing with another Temperament.

INSTRUCTIONS FOR TAKING THE TEMPERAMENT TEST

This test that follows is to determine the emotional, behavioral and cognitive aspects. In each of the four columns you will find a list of possible strengths and weaknesses of your Temperament. Read each one and place a number from 1 to 5 next to the word. Once completed, add up your overall scores, crossing out any word that you placed a 1 or 2 before. Then add up the 3s, 4s and 5s. Write this total at the bottom of the appropriate section. The column with your highest score is your Primary Temperament and if your second largest score is a significant number, it is your Secondary Temperament. We are all a blend of the various natures. There is no perfect score, just a tendency to one or the other.

HOW TO SCORE YOUR ANSWERS

1 = definitely not me
2 = usually not me
3 = usually me
4 = mostly me
5 = definitely me

The Temperament Test

Section 1 Earthy (Cold/Dry)	Section 2 Airy (Hot/Wet)	Section 3 Fiery (Hot/Dry)	Section 4 Watery (Cold/Wet)

Strengths

—— stable	—— communicative	—— inspiring	—— good feelings
—— organized	—— quick-witted	—— active	—— imaginative
—— predictable	—— adaptable	—— enthusiastic	—— creative
—— disciplined	—— versatile	—— passionate	—— sensitive
—— responsible	—— flexible	—— charismatic	—— sympathetic
—— reliable	—— pleasant	—— spontaneous	—— domestic
—— practical	—— cooperative	—— gut-level instinct	—— compassionate
—— realistic	—— sociable	—— self-confident	—— benevolent
—— hardworking	—— adventurous	—— extroverted	—— intuitive
—— ambitious	—— tolerant	—— keen intellect	—— artistic
—— analytical	—— original	—— optimistic	—— receptive
—— methodical	—— experience life	—— risk-taker	—— tranquil
—— steady	—— storyteller	—— assertive	—— healing force
—— sensual	—— interpreter	—— individualistic	—— unite people
—— loves tangible	—— journalist	—— self-expressive	—— emotional
—— persistent	—— many friends	—— dramatic	—— loves feeling right
—— thoughtful	—— curious	—— self-motivated	—— value things
—— sensible	—— freedom loving	—— fun loving	—— introspective
—— dependable	—— link ideas, places	—— independent	—— romantic

Weaknesses

—— rigid	—— talk too much	—— willful	—— moody
—— loner	—— nervous	—— impatient	—— clingy
—— stubborn	—— superficial	—— reactive	—— secretive
—— lazy	—— indecisive	—— blunt	—— escapist
—— reserved	—— aloof	—— careless	—— impractical
—— critical	—— eccentric	—— foolish	—— unrealistic
—— pessimistic	—— impersonal	—— brash	—— brooding
—— suspicious	—— disorganized	—— impulsive	—— manipulative
—— moody	—— detached	—— boisterous	—— boundaries lost
—— materialistic	—— too theoretical	—— love flattery	—— sensitive
—— easy to control	—— procrastinator	—— dislike ignored	—— see emotionally
—— conservative	—— emotional	—— gullible	—— impractical
—— cautious	—— unfocused	—— proud	—— irrational
—— workaholic	—— dispassionate	—— headstrong	—— depressed
—— hoarder	—— remote	—— unaffectionate	—— vulnerable
—— withdrawn	—— insensitive	—— insensitive	—— self-protective
—— lack imagination	—— analyze things	—— argumentative	—— ultra sensitive
—— fixed on rules	—— too abstract	—— domineering	—— impressionable
—— hard to please	—— dreamer	—— intolerant	—— compulsive
—— indecisive	—— lazy	—— stubborn	—— callous

Now you can match your Temperament with the foods that you consume. If you determine from the Temperament Test that you exhibit some of the weaknesses of your temperament, changes may occur through correcting your diet, as the weaknesses indicate bad humours.If you have a hot temperament and it becomes out of balance, your diet should consist of cold-tempered foods and vice versa. This is why it is essential that you know the Temperament of the foods that you eat.

You may also take our Temperament Test online at:

www.avicennacuisine.com

CHAPTER 24

The Imbalanced Temperament

THE SIMPLE IMBALANCED TEMPERAMENTS ARE where there is an active opposite quality (hot or cold-tempered) that is in excess. That is, the temperament is hotter than it should be, not moister or drier. This is called hot imbalanced temperament. Or the temperament may be colder than it should be, not moister or drier. This is known as cold imbalanced temperament.

Where there is a passive contrary quality (moist or dry) that is in excess the temperament may be drier than it should be, but not hotter nor colder. This is dry imbalanced temperament.

Or the temperament may be moister than it should be, but not hotter nor colder. This is called moist imbalanced temperament. Simple imbalances do not, however, last long, as they tend to be soon converted into compound imbalances. That is, an imbalance in the direction of excessive heat promptly leads to dryness and a change in the direction of cold increases the moisture. Dryness no doubt quickly increases cold in the body, but moisture, provided it is excessive, makes it much more cold. If, however, the increase of moisture is moderately cold, it would appear only after some considerable time. From this it will be seen that heat is generally more favorable than cold for maintaining the proper balance and general health of our body.

HOT IMBALANCED TEMPERAMENT

THE THINGS THAT PRODUCE HEAT

A hot imbalanced temperament can be caused by the following: (1) External heat in various forms: summer heat, artificial heat, baths of moderate temperature (the heating effect is produced by both air and water). (2) Heat produced by movement such as exercise, but not in excess or gymnastic exercise that is not too vigorous or beyond the right measure and duration; moderate friction and light massage with our hands on the limbs. (3) Heat introduced by the mouth with an adequate supply of nutriment, hot aliments, hot or heating medicines (such as via oxidation with our body). (4) Heat arising from our emotional states such as anger, depression in a degree less than would cause cooling and moderated joy. Our sleep and wakefulness can also be a moderate factor. (5) Heat that is derived from putrefaction. This is neither the Innate Heat or heat derived from combustion. The warming from the Innate Heat is less in degree than that from combustion. It can occur apart from putrefaction and prior to a diseased state. In the case of putrefaction, the heat from the foreign source lingers in our body after the agent giving rise to it has left our body. This heat unites with the moisture of the humours and alters our temperament (in respect of moisture) in such a manner that it will no longer respond to the temperament of the natural breath.[37]

Heat eliminates unnecessary and unknown materials found in the body to cleanse and restore the spirit. This occurs when heat uses its natural forces to open up channels and pores to eliminate impurities. At the same time, heat thins out our bodily fluids, which allow US to evacuate through opened channels. This explains why your nose will start to run after eating a spicy bowl of chili. Heat also burns up toxins and helps speed up metabolism and digestion, which aid in evacuating waste materials from the body.

Warmth Produced from Hot-Tempered Foods

In ancient times many considered a healthy body to be warm in the first degree. Ingredients that "are hot in the first degree, are of equal heath with our bodies, and they only add a natural heat thereto, if it be cooled by nature or by accident, thereby cherishing the natural heat when weak, and restoring it when it is wanting."[38] In other words, every person has an Inner Heat within them that eliminates impurities and toxins from the body as stated above. When we eat foods that are hot to the first degree, we create warmth throughout the body, which is healthy and good.

Heating Ingredients

First Degree Heat: These ingredients "decrease inflammations and fevers by opening the pores of the skin"[39] to let out chill and blockage that has invaded the body, returning it to its normal temperature. These foods are mainly calming diaphoretics such as Carrots, Chamomile, Fenugreek Leaks, Potatoes, and Peppermint.

Second Degree Heat: This heat is similar to the first degree heat and opens even more pores and channels, while dissolving irregular humours so that fluids are able to flow through openings and be released from the body. These foods are mainly warming bitters: Basil, Cardamom, Cinnamon, Fennel, Dried Ginger, Mint, Nutmeg, Saffron and Turmeric.

Third Degree Heat: Ingredients that produce third degree heat blend with our Innate Heat to push liquefied fluids, toxins and impurities to the surface and out through open pores and channels. They "help concoction," that is, cooking in the stomach, warm and comfort the viscera, and "keep the blood in its just temperature."[40] These ingredients are primarily cleansers and stimulants such as Black Pepper, Cabbage, Cayenne Pepper, Cumin and Fresh Ginger.

Fourth Degree Heat: This heat is the most severe and can be poisonous. If rubbed on our skin, these ingredients will cause blisters and potentially burn the skin. When ingested, more gentle ingredients like black mustard are used as a remedy to stimulate blood flow to undernourished and under stimulated areas. On the contrary, more severe ingredients in this degree are used as remedies to remove unfamiliar growths such as warts and cancers. Examples are: Nettle, Black Mustard, Garlic, Onion, Savory, and Chelidonium.

ON THE SIGNS OF A HOT IMBALANCED TEMPERAMENT

- Thirst is a sign of a hot imbalanced temperament, as well as:
- Smoky flavored belching; and
- Saliva in our mouth that smells like meat and sweat.
- We like cold foods and drinks and they help relieve our symptoms.
- The burning of gentle food in the stomach that would not normally burn in a stomach with a natural temperament.
- Thick and heavy foods digest more quickly than in a stomach with a natural temperament. This only occurs if the hot imbalanced temperament is not so extreme as to destroy the stomach's powers and weaken and disable it.
- Being very thirsty and most of the time not having an appetite for food can particularly be the case with extreme yellow bile humour and a hot imbalanced temperament of our stomach. It destroys our appetite completely, but the strength of digestion is still intact unless this hot imbal-

anced temperament reaches its last stage and disables our digestion system.

- Sometimes we have a hot imbalanced temperament and feel hungry before losing our appetite. This is due to the fact that heat from our imbalanced temperament destroys nutrients inside our stomach.
- With hunger caused by a hot imbalanced temperament, saliva drips from our mouth and does not stop until food reaches our stomach. This is because dissolving heat for food leaves our stomach and comes up, and while coming up, it dries up the source of the secretion of saliva. It is possible that introducing a great enough amount of thick food into our stomach will prevent saliva from being secreted.
- A wet hot imbalanced temperament in our stomach causes more saliva from our mouth when our mouth has a dry imbalanced temperament.
- The blood humour of those of us who have a hot imbalanced temperament in the stomach is strong-tasting, has a bad smell and indicates anemia. Other organs in the body with a different temperament from that of our stomach repel this blood humour. They will not accept it and therefore have no other source of nutrition.
- A person with a hot imbalanced temperament in the stomach is known to be thin.

ON THE DIET FOR A HOT IMBALANCED TEMPERAMENT

If the heat has not reached the level at which it decreases our strength and makes us tired, we should eat thick cooling foods including fresh fish and anything that is astringent.

COLD IMBALANCED TEMPERAMENT

THE THINGS THAT PRODUCE COLD

The causes of a cold imbalanced temperament are: (1) Artificial cold, or cooling in act, such as a spa experience in the ice room. (2) When our body is hot and then exposed to a cooling agent, its heat becomes dissipated like thermal waters. (3) Cooling agents that are excessive, for example very hot air, thermal waters, hot plasters and fermentations (which disperse the Innate Heat by relaxing the body); or moderate as in staying too long in the bath, or agents one time hot, but becoming cold later. (4)

Excessive exercise, which disperses the Innate Heat unduly. Excessive sleep aggregates and strangles our Innate Heat, thereby having a cooling effect. (5) Certain bodily states. Great decrease in density relaxes the body and disperses our Innate Heat; extreme density, thickness and compactness strangles our Innate Heat; excessive retention (has the same action); undue evacuation from our body destroys the material basis of the Innate Heat and disperses the breath, which allows the effete matters to become obstructions. (6) Mental states. Great gloom, too much fear, too much joy, great delight. (7) Aliment. Excess of food and drink, cold aliments, too little food, refrigerant medicines. (8) Mechanical causes. Tight bandaging of limbs for some time that prevents our Innate Heat reaching them. (9) Crudity, the opposite of putrefaction.

COOLING PRODUCED FROM COLD-TEMPERED FOODS

It is essential that we have cold-tempered ingredients because cold binds together things harmonious or unharmonious. Therefore, when cold is absent from the body, the different parts of the body begin to detach and flow alone.

COOLING INGREDIENTS

"Observe, that those foods that are called cold, are not so called because that they are really cold in themselves, but because the degree of their heat falls below the heat of our bodies, and so only in respect of our temperature are said to be cold."[41] Cold ingredients calm the body, mind and spirit; similar to when rapid boiling water is settled by turning down the heat. This can also explain why cold ingredients calm down nervousness, anxiety and these kinds of conditions where energy begins to rise out of control.

First Degree Cold: Ingredients cold in the first degree "qualify the heat of the stomach, cause digestion" and "refresh the spirits."[42] Many fresh fruits and vegetables are cold in the first degree. The cooling sensation makes one feel refreshed and less stuffy and bothered on a hot summer day. Examples: Beets, Cucumber, Mushrooms, Lemon, Olives, Parsley, Peach, Rose Petals, Tomato and Zucchini.

Second Degree Cold: These ingredients are primarily anti-inflammatory, or "refrigerants." Examples include Beef, Lime, Lettuce, Squash, Pumpkin and Strawberry.

Third Degree Cold: Ingredients that are cold to the third degree help to reduce sweating and perspiration caused by too much heat from physical exercise or stressful conditions such as nervousness. Thee ingredients also help keep internal vapors from rising, which reduces the chance of restlessness and fainting. Examples include Lavender, Poppy Flowers, and Watermelon.

Fourth Degree Cold: These ingredients are typically drugs and substances that are used as remedies for extreme pain. When ingested these mild to powerful sedatives or poisons can result in unconsciousness. Examples are Wild Lettuce, Opium and Hemlock.

ON THE SIGNS OF A COLD IMBALANCED TEMPERAMENT

- The conversion and digestion of food in our stomach is slow. The food reaches our stomach later than normal and is not completely digested or:
- Excess appetite for food;
- Less feeling thirsty; and
- Sour belching, unless the sour belch is from the food.
- People with a cold imbalanced temperament enjoy eating light and watery foods and can digest them easily. They are not able to digest food as thick as the food they used to digest before acquiring a cold imbalanced temperament.
- This cold imbalanced temperament can reach a level that causes the stomach to stretch. There is also an extra disturbance to the stomach for some time just a few hours after food enters the stomach. This stretching and disturbance does not go away until the stomach releases some moisture with food and it passes through the stomach. The stomach will then be relieved of the stretching. A very extreme cold imbalanced temperament can cause corruption of the stomach and edema.
- Other organs can be a cause of this cold imbalanced temperament. For example, if our brain is one part of the causes, a person will have headaches from gas and hear sounds such as humming or buzzing.
- If we are among those who have a naturally hot imbalanced temperament and cold imbalanced temperament mixes with that in us, the signs are stomach-rumbling, stomach gas, tongue dryness, and a great deal of thirst. Overall this causes a very bad feeling.

ON THE DIET FOR A COLD IMBALANCED TEMPERAMENT

- Drinking Red Wine is a good way to warm our stomach. If it causes hiccups and this indicates that it was helpful.
- Put more Black Pepper in our food, which also causes warmth.
- Sleeping has a great deal of benefit for a cold imbalanced temperament and it is better than anything else.
- Oils that can be rubbed and used on a cold imbalanced temperament include: Camomile Oil, Henna Oil, Iris Oil, and Mastic Oil that has to be mixed with Chicken Fat. If we want the Mastic Oil to be more helpful and beneficial, add Desert Thumb and Jewish-Meccan Bdellium to it in addition to Chicken Fat.
- From among the seeds—they are beneficial in treating this condition— use Fenugreek, Celery and Hollyhock Seeds.

DRY IMBALANCED TEMPERAMENT

THE THINGS WHICH PRODUCE DRYNESS (DESICCANTS)

The causes of a dry imbalanced temperament are: (1) External— cold congeals the humours and prevents the tissues from attracting nutritive material. It also constricts the channels of our body and because so, causes them to be blocked; in consequence nutrient material cannot reach it. (2) Great heat which disperses moisture. Therefore, too frequent hot baths have this effect. (3) Bathing in waters that contract tissue to seal injured blood vessels that has a drying effect. (4) Diet—insufficient food, dry aliments, drying medicines; (5) Violent evacuations and coitus; (6) Excessive exercise;(7) Excessive wakefulness; (8) Frequent emotional disturbance.

DRYING QUALITIES PRODUCED IN DRY-TEMPERED FOODS

The dry quality creates a structure for each and every ingredient and substance to live, separate from one another. Dryness is also responsible for holding anything we eat, drink and breath within our bodies. In the first degree, the dry quality protects the ingredient from outside influences. In the fourth degree, it hardens the substance completely.

Drying Ingredients

"Drying ingredients are such as make dry the parts overflowing with moisture"[43] and "drying ingredients consume the humours, stop fluxes, stiffen the parts, and strengthen nature."[44] We can mainly categorize dry ingredients as liquid contained astringents or alkaline remedies that restore the depleted mineral content of electrolytes in water.

First Degree Dry: Opposite of first degree warm ingredients, first degree dry ingredients close pores instead of opening them and keep the body from catching cold sicknesses in the winter. These ingredients are said to "comfort and strengthen nature."[45] A few examples are Beef, Sweet Fern, Mushrooms, Leeks, Ledum Camphor, Saffron and Sumac.

Second Degree Dry: Similar to first degree dry ingredients, second degree dry also comforts and strengthens nature. For instance, this degree binds body tissues together to support them so they do not become weak and fall apart. These would be astringents such as Black-Eyed Peas, Cardamom, Cinnamon, Celery, Cabbage, Garlic, Mint, Oak, Onions, Radish and Raspberry Leaf.

Third Degree Dry: Ingredients dry to the third degree strengthen nature, bind body tissues together, and stop the release of body fluids. These are astringents such as Basil, Blueberry Leaf, Cloves, White Pepper and Waterlily.

Fourth Degree Dry: These harden the tissues to resist consumptions of fluxes of blood, humours, and catarrhs. Avicenna used Rose Petals, a dry ingredient to the fourth degree, to heal tubercular bleeding and expel coughing and spitting from the throat and lungs.

On the Signs of a Dry Imbalanced Temperament

- A great deal of thirst
- Tongue dryness that it is much drier than normal
- Losing weight and feeling weak more than normal
- We enjoy wet-tempered foods and a wet and humid weather

On the Diet for a Dry Imbalanced Temperament

- Drink milk. The best milk in treating a dry imbalanced temperament is cow's Milk. Drink it as fresh and organic as possible. Do not eat very much at all until this milk has digested. Eat lightly and drink milk again four hours later.

- Avoid rich, hard, viscous and clammy foods.
- We need to drink plenty of water.
- Drink wine that has an astringent taste. This Wine is helpful for the treatment of a moist-tempered stomach.
- Eat light foods to avoid having a second meal reach the first one before it is completely digested.

WET IMBALANCED TEMPERAMENT

THE THINGS THAT PRODUCE MOISTURE

The causes of moisture are: (1) Bathing directly after a meal; (2) Diet—overeating moist articles of food and taking moist medications; (3) Retention of that which should be evacuated; (4) Evacuation of dry humour; (5) Excessive sleep; (6) Joy in moderation; (7) Infrigidants (these cause the humours to be retained); and (8) Calefacients (a slight degree of warmth causes the humours to move).

MOISTURE PRODUCED FROM WET-TEMPERED FOODS

Ingredients with a wet quality are lubricating and flow freely without friction against other substances. The wet quality is nourishing because the food can travel through fluids when digested and get to the tissues to feed them the nutrients. Consuming foods with a wet temperament moisten surfaces, moisten organs, and revives hardened tissues.

MOISTURE PRODUCING INGREDIENTS

First Degree Moist: These ingredients moisten the windpipe and act on the mucus of the respiratory tract to reduce coughing and dryness. Examples are Beets, Figs, Thin Green Beans, Lamb, Marsh Mallow Root, Pears, Turnips and Potatoes.

Second Degree Moist: These ingredients moisten the windpipe and act on the mucus of the digestive tract to loosen the stomach, moisten channels and stimulate evacuation. They also moisten the stool and help in nurturing the womb to promote fertility and birth. Wet ingredients in the second degree feature Asparagus, Butternut Squash, Carrots, Chicken,

Green Beans, Lettuce, Lima Beans and Zucchini.

Third Degree Moist: As we increase to the third grade of wetness, we discover that these ingredients moisten the body and calm body parts that are feeling tight or stiff. Examples include Marsh Mallow Root, Common Comfrey and Fenugreek.

Fourth Degree Moist: This level of moistness provides lubrication to the stool to remove stuck bowels when our kidneys are not working properly. They are laxatives, and ingredients that accelerate defecation. Examples include Yellow Dock Root, Rhubarb Root, Sacred Bark, Senna and Poke Root.

ON THE SIGNS OF A WET IMBALANCED TEMPERAMENT

- Less feeling of thirst.
- We dislike moist-tempered foods. They sicken us.
- We feel good after eating something.
- Excess saliva. If we have a lot of saliva when we are hungry, this is from heat that comes with a wet imbalanced temperament. Most of the time, heat and wet temperaments together are sources of excess saliva.
- After eating and after the food enters our stomach, we feel that if we move or walk around, the food will come up. This is sign of a wet imbalanced temperament that is not disabled. This feeling also can happen with hunger or before our stomach is filled with enough food. But with hunger, if we begin eating food and as soon as we begin eating, we start having the same feeling; otherwise this feeling does not occur in hunger without beginning to eat.

ON THE DIET FOR A WET IMBALANCED TEMPERAMENT

- Food for those of us with a wet imbalanced temperament need to be dry-tempered foods without any broth or sauces.
- It is better to drink less liquids during the imbalanced time period.

SUMMARY OF EVIDENCE OF THE IMBALANCED TEMPERAMENTS

As we have said, understanding our temperament and the temperament of the foods we eat is essentially important to maintaining balance and health in our body and mind. Avicenna Cuisine will teach you how to select foods that suit you best and bring you to an equable state. For example, we mentioned in chapter one that phlegmatic tempered individuals are cold and wet. Therefore these individuals should avoid cold and wet foods and drinks and select foods that are hot and dry. The same goes for the other three humours and temperaments. We should practice eating and drinking the opposite temperament of ourselves to create balance.

In regard to foods and medicines with a hot imbalanced temperament, heating agents are all harmful while cooling agents benefit; with a cold imbalanced temperament, cooling agents are all harmful while heating agents benefit; with a moist imbalanced temperament, moist articles of diet are harmful; with a dry imbalanced temperament, dry regime is harmful while moist articles of diet are beneficial.

Now we turn to a further understanding of how to determine the temperament of the food and drink that we consume.

Part V

The Temperament of Simple Foods

USING TASTE TO BALANCE YOUR TEMPERAMENT

TEMPERAMENT	BALANCED TASTES	IRRITABLE TASTES
EARTH (COLD/DRY)	Bitter, Salty, Pungent (Hot)	Acrid, Biting, Sour (Cold)
AIR (HOT/WET)	Acrid, Biting, Sour (Cold)	Bitter, Salty, Pungent (Hot)
FIRE (HOT/DRY)	Acrid, Biting, Sour (Cold)	Bitter, Salty, Pungent (Hot)
WATER (COLD/WET)	Bitter, Salty, Pungent (Hot)	Acrid, Biting, Sour (Cold)

CHAPTER 25

Determining the Temperament of Simple Foods

WE HAVE MENTIONED HOW THE NATURAL QUALITIES of foods relate to our bodies. We have also stated that all the vegetable, mineral and animal compounds are based on the four elements of earth, air, fire and water. Each of these has two natural qualities, namely: earth is cold and wet, air is hot and wet, fire is hot and dry, and water is cold and wet. These natural qualities are referred to as a food's temperament. When these natural qualities inter-mingle, its temperament either remains balanced or one natural quality dominates over another one. When one of the natural qualities is in balance, it is called the food's real temperament.When a food takes on a tempera-ment, it receives the energy or powers that are inherent to that tempera-ment.

What is a balanced temperament in human beings as well as a bal-anced temperament in foods? Whenever a food comes in contact with the human body and its Innate Heat, the Innate Heat of the body influences the food so that which is hot becomes cold and that which is dry becomes wet or it is transformed in the reverse. We are not saying that the temperament of a food is the same as the human temperament. The human temperament is exclusive to itself.

There are two levels of temperament. The first temperament emerges from the four natural qualities mentioned above. Examples of the second temperament are compound foods or antidotes. Their tempera-ments arise from the mixture of natural qualities.

Therefore, every simple healing food that is used as an antidote has a temperament that is unshared. When simple healing foods are put to-gether to form a compound, the temperament of the compound food is re-ferred to as a secondary temperament. This, then, is an acquired, secondary temperament. However, this secondary temperament is not always acquired or artificial, it may also be natural. In fact, milk is a mixture of water, cheese and butter. Each one of them, again, is not simple by nature. Each one is a compound having its own temperament. In the case of milk, its secondary temperament comes from nature rather than being acquired or artificial.

There are many simple foods when eaten produce intense cold be-cause of their transformation from washing. When used as a poultice, how-ever, they act as dissolvents (indicating a hot temperament). Coriander is an example. It generates intense cold when taken orally. However, when used to wrap or bind a body with it, it dissolves swellings. This is especially so when it is mixed with the meal of barley or wheat.

The reason for this is that coriander consists of two foods: an in-tensely cold, moist property and a moderately hot or diluting (rarefying, at-tenuant) property. Used orally, Innate Heat rises up and dissolves the finer food. Its diluting property does not remain in any quantity to affect the tem-perament. As it disperses into the body, it is almost completely eliminated. Its cold property remains when it is used in the form of a poultice. This is due to the fact that its cold property is not able to move through the pores.

Yet the fine, hot food moves through the pores of the body and maturates it. If some of the cold property combines with it, the mixture may prove to be useful in repelling the external heat.

This is what we have described in Volume 1 relating to the onion. The onion causes a sensation of burning when it is used as a poultice. However, it is very safe when eaten orally.

Therefore, in conclusion, there are some foods that appear to have two foods of differing temperaments. An example of those opposing natural qualities that are perceptible is the citron.

Then there are those opposite natural qualities that remain more invisible. An example of this would be psyllium husk seeds. Psyllium husk seeds have strong cooling properties. However, when a flour is made, the flour has strong heating properties to the extent that it may produce skin-redness (indicating a hot temperament). If the husks are taken unbroken, their hard covering will not allow this hidden property to act and produce ulcers. They will only act with the properties of its husk. However, if it is powdered and flour made, it will most likely act as a poison. It is believed that this is caused by its hidden properties. This is why powdered psyllium husks may open abscesses, yet the intact husks repel decaying or decomposing foods from it without allowing these decaying or decomposing food to grow.

Tastes, Odors, Colors

Taste is more important than color or odor in determining the temperament of a food because taste is felt when it is actually in physical contact with a person, not just present to their senses. This is the best way of determining a food's temperament. Odor and color show their temperament when they are not in physical contact, but in sensory contact. It may be that vapors arise from the diluting part of a food, yet no vapor arises from the heavy part of the food. A color that is perceptible may be the color of the exterior and not the color of the interior. An odor may indicate taste. Examples are sweet, sour, pungent or bitter odors. All these odors follow taste. This indicates how taste is the most precise indication of the nature of a food, then odor and, finally, color. It should be noted that foods that have a deep color, definite taste and distinct smell are stronger.

TASTES

If taste were not the most important indication of temperament, opium would not have tasted bitter in spite of the fact that it is extremely cold. It is not the case that a discrepancy in taste is more easily determined with a cold than with a hot food. It may be that a taste that appears to be warm is, in reality, cold. On the other hand, a food that indicates cold is often hot. This is because a hot food is generally more active and impressive. If a hot temperament interacts with a cold temperament, the power of the hot temperament could suffice to dissipate the cold effect of the other. The taste of the first would suppress the taste of the latter because a hot food dominates as does its taste and odor. This is why it would be very rare to find a hot food that is sour and astringent and having no temperament. However, a cold food could be bitter and irritating in taste. While this may happen often, it is not an absolute rule.

Tastes are classified into nine types—eight real and the ninth being tasteless. An example of a tasteless food would be water. Nutritionists agree that taste is a sensation that is immediately felt. It can never be passive. There is no such thing as a passive taste.

Explaining the classification of tastes, nutritionists state that a food would be either dense, tenuous or moderate in its attributes depending upon its taste. In terms of temperament, the potency of its taste would indicate that the food was either hot, cold or moderate.

TASTES INDICATING A COLD TEMPERAMENT

1   Acrid: cold temperament; if weak, it is astringent; if strong, it has the power to apply pressure.
2   Biting: cold temperament; a biting taste indicates a food will be constipating as well as thickening and hardening.
3   Sour: cold temperament; a sour taste indicates a food will be cooling. All sour foods are opening (deobstruent).

An acrid taste indicates the coldest temperament. Fruits are first acrid, astringent, sour and, finally, sweet. At the first stage they are extremely cold. Its coldness stems from its acidity. As air and water pass through it and, in most cases, it receives sunlight, its taste is transformed into sourness. An example would be sour grapes. Between its acidity and sourness, a bit of biting taste develops as it loses its acrid taste. Its temperament then transforms into sweetness due to the heat it has received from the sun.

TASTES INDICATING A COLD NATURE

Taste	Description	Foods
Acrid	An acrid taste indicates the coldest nature and is sharp and cutting. Fruits are first acrid, biting, sour and finally, sweet. As air and water pass through it and in most cases, it receives sunlight, its taste is transformed into sourness. Acrid is similar to a biting taste except it penetrates both the interior of the tongue and the surface.	Unripened Fruit (Grapes, Olives, Berries)
Biting	A biting taste is piercing, sharp and stinging and indicates a food will be constipating, thickening, hardening and retentive. Similar to an acrid taste except biting tastes only bite the surface of the tongue.	Radishes Horseradish
Sour	A sour taste is acidic and tart and indicates that a food will be cooling and lacerating. All sour foods are opening (of obstructions).	Apple Grape Lemon Mango Pineapple Tomato Vinegar

It is possible that some fruits do not pass through the sour stage. An example is the olive. The coldness of the taste of sour fruit is less than its acrid taste. But in most cases, due to its tenuousness that passes through its acridity, its taste becomes colder than acrid. Acridity and biting tastes are tastes that are similar to each other. The difference is that a biting taste bites the surface of the tongue while the acrid penetrates both the interior of the tongue and the surface.

An acrid taste irritates externally. It indicates that a food is dense and unable to split into minute particles swiftly and because different parts of the food join each other rapidly. Due to these two conditions, the effect of an acrid taste varies from one part of the tongue to the other. However, the parts of the tongue differ in density. This also helps acridity in its action.

Although sourness indicates a less cold temperament than an acrid taste does, it is mainly colder because of the presence of tenuousness. An acrid taste is sharper and more penetrating.

TASTES INDICATING A HOT TEMPERAMENT

4   Bitter: hot temperament; a bitter taste indicates a food will be cleansing and coarsening. All bitter foods are tenuous and opening (deobstruent).
5   Salty: hot temperament; a salty taste indicates a food will be cleansing, dilutant, drying and resistant to putrefaction.
6   Pungent: hot temperament; a pungent taste indicates a food will be dissolving, lacerating and putrefying. All pungent foods are opening (deobstruent).
7   Greasy: heating temperament; a greasy taste indicates a food will be softening, sliding and slightly maturating.
8   Sweet: heating temperament; a sweet taste indicates a food will be ripening, softening and nutritious.

A pungent taste is hotter than a bitter or salty taste. Because of this, it indicates that a food is more capable of dissolving, diluting and cleansing.

A bitter taste is stronger than a salty taste. This is because it is a salty-bitter taste due to the presence of some moisture so that its inherent property has been reduced. In this transformation, it has lost some of its heat.

TASTES INDICATING A HOT NATURE

Taste	Description	Foods
Bitter	A bitter taste is heavy, dry, sharp and stronger than a salty taste. Bitter tastes indicate that a food will be cleansing and coarsening. All bitter foods are blood thinning and opening (of obstructions).	Arugula Broccoli Coffee Dill Grapefruit Leafy Vegetables Turmeric Vinegar Wine
Salty	A salty taste indicates a food will be cleansing, diluting, drying and resistant to decay. In regard to a salty taste, it was first bitter. A salty substance turns out to be bitter because of the warmth of the sun or fire or because of the disappearance of moisture that causes a reduction in the degree of heat.	Capers Fish Miso Natural Salts Olives Oysters Seaweed Soy Sauce Sea Vegetables
Pungent	A pungent taste is spicy and hot and indicates that a food will be dissolving, lacerating and resistant to decay. All pungent foods are opening (of obstructions). Pungent tastes are hotter and stronger than a bitter or salty taste, which makes them more capable of dissolving, diluting and cleansing.	Chives Parsley Chillies Mustard Garlic Ginger Fennel Green Onion

TASTES INDICATING A HOT NATURE...

Taste	Description	Foods
Greasy	A greasy taste indicates a food will be softening, sliding and slightly maturating. Greasy foods give pleasure to the tongue and lubricate it, facilitating the food to smoothly liquefy. A greasy taste removes dryness of the tongue.	French Fries Onion Rings Hamburgers Fried Foods Pizza Donuts
Sweet	A sweet taste is sugary and honeyed and indicates a food will be ripening, softening and nutritive. Similar to greasy foods, sweet foods give pleasure to the tongue and lubricate it, facilitating the food to smoothly liquefy. These foods also remove dryness of the tongue and create a warming effect.	Apple Banana Natural Sugars Carrot Chicken Coconut Pumpkin Saffron Shrimp Watermelon Wine

In regard to a salty taste, it was first bitter. A salty food turns out to be bitter because of the warmth of the sun or fire or because of the disappearance of moisture that causes a reduction in the degree of heat. As far as a salty food is concerned, if it appears to be bitter, its heat has been dissipated by its cold and moist nature. Among the salts, a bitter salt is warmer than an edible salt.

Both pungent and bitter tastes scratch the tongue with one difference. While the pungent goes deeper because it is substantially sharp and penetrating, the bitter scratches the surface alone because it is heavy and dry. A purely bitter taste is neither capable of accepting a stench that can produce germs nor does it provide food for them. It is because of its dryness that the bitter tastes have a coarse scathing effect.

One of the causes why the heat of a pungent taste is stronger than that of bitter taste is that the pungent taste is so piercing that it causes severe damage and discomfort to the tongue, almost to the extent of corroding and putrefying, which sometimes results in the destruction of the tissue.

Bitter and salty tastes cause some irritation to the tongue. A salty taste affects slightly, washes the tongue and does not bring about coarseness. A salty taste is tenuous and reaches all parts of the body. It spreads evenly to all parts of the body. However, its taste harms the orifice of the stomach. Bitterness causes severe irritation. This results in coarseness due to its diverse action.

A salty taste is formed when something bitter is diluted with something tasteless like water. This, when congealed, like an alkaline solution, becomes salty.

Both the sweet and greasy tastes give pleasure to the tongue and lubricate it, facilitating the food to smoothly liquefy. Sweet and greasy foods remove coarseness of the tongue. While a greasy taste removes coarseness of the tongue without perceptible heating, sweetness does the same with a warming effect. That is why sweetness is more ripening.

A sweet taste changes a dense food by cleansing, softening, generating fluidity and removing the density without eroding it, while correcting loss of continuity without causing irritation. It produces a heat that is not harmful, but pleasing such as the soothing effect of warm water poured over the back. Although a sweet taste is delicious and cleansing, it is not always nourishing.

A greasy taste is consistent with sweetness. Nevertheless, a dense food cooked into something that is sweet or greasy would transform the ingredient into sweetness if the tenuousness of the food was based on the presence of moisture and a little of airiness. If the tenuousness of the food is due to its pure moisture and air content, it will tend to be greasy and intervene as it is very much prone towards producing moistness.

MIXED HOT AND COLD TASTES

A pungent and sour taste causes irritation to the tongue. The pungent irritates it with severe inflammation and the sour acts moderately without inflammation.

A biting taste and a sour taste both irritate the tongue, but a biting taste is more irritating and brings heat. A sour taste bites the tongue but not to a great extent. It may even say to be moderate and it is not followed by any heat. When a food that has a biting taste is boiled, due to its moisture and humidity, and its moisture and humidity is not enough to change its actions, it creates sourness if the food is generally sour.

When a sweet tasting food is boiled, due to its moisture and humidity, and its moisture and humidity are not enough to change its actions, it creates sweetness if the food is generally sweet, but any bitterness and biting effect indicates that the food is closer to dryness.

A sour taste is formed by the transformation of a sour taste into a sweet taste due to lack of heat or by the maturity of acridity due to abundance of moisture and heat. The temperament of a sour taste, in any case, is moist.

A sweet taste is formed by its transformation due to lack of heat or by the maturity of acridity due to abundance of moisture and heat. The temperament of a sweet tastes tends towards humidity, whereas the bitter and acrid tastes tend toward dryness.

WHEN TWO OR MORE TASTES COMBINE IN ONE FOOD

If bitterness and a biting taste combine in, for example, the extract of the barberry plant, the taste thus produced is described as being unpleasant. It is said to be similar to the brininess of bitter, salty water in arid ground.

The tastes of bitterness and saltiness combine in cinnamon.

The tastes of pungency and sweetness combine in honey.

Bitter, pungent and biting tastes combine in eggplant.

Bitterness and tastelessness combine in wild endive.

WHEN TWO OR MORE TASTES COMBINE TOGETHER, THERE MAY BE AN ADDITIONAL EFFECT

When there is a mixture of sour and biting tastes as in sour grapes, its biting taste does not allow its sourness to penetrate a great deal.

WHERE A NATURAL QUALITY IS A HELPER OR VEHICLE

Tastes of pungency and bitterness co-exist in vinegar in a larger degree than in wine. This makes vinegar very cold since these two tastes open up pores enabling the cold effect to be felt. If they have not reached a considerably warm stage, the cold effect of vinegar would be more intense.

Mixing foods may as a corrective for foods and remove their harmful effects. Foods that are destroyed are foods that have a mild purgative quality. It needs the help of something to be added to it. When, for example, a helping food such as turpeth root, is added to epithyme, it heightens its property. Turpeth has a weak purgative quality. It is not capable of dissolving in a strong way. Therefore, it removes what is thin in the serous humour, but when dried ginger is added to it, due to the intensity of dried ginger, epithyme quickly evacuates a humour that is highly viscous and moist. In the case with epithyme, it is a food that is slow in purgation. When epithyme is mixed with pepper and other tenuous foods, it swiftly purgates. It then helps in dissolution.

Rhubarb, as another example, has a strong astringent and, at the same time, an opening property that corrupts its action. When mixed with Armenian bole or wild gum Arabic tree, it creates an even more severe constipation.

Sometimes the mixing of foods is done to allow them to penetrate or serve as a vehicle. An example is that of saffron mixed with rose, camphor or coral. This makes it more affective in penetrating to the heart.

WHEN TWO OR MORE TASTES PREVENTS THE TASTE OF INDIVIDUAL NATURAL QUALITIES TO BE PERCEIVED

An example is when sour and acrid tastes combine in sour grapes. This prevents the sour taste from developing a severe, penetrating, cooling effect.

WHEN THE NATURAL QUALITIES ARE OPPOSITES

An example is that of yogurt such that the thickness that appears in yogurt when the water is drained out and the cold of that reaches the lowest possible.

Sometimes foods are mixed for an opposite purpose. As an example, take radish seeds. When radish seeds are mixed with penetrating, diluting foods, this is done so that the radish seeds will be retained by the liver until the objective of their use is achieved. The objective will be lost if the tenuous foods penetrate the liver before the desired action is obtained.

Radish seeds create a tendency to vomiting. With their opposite action, they obstruct absorption by the veins.

Foods that loose their properties on being mixed with other foods are those that hold a healing property in common, but other properties that are opposite or nearly opposite. If on mixing of two foods, one dominates the other, the action would be done, but if it does not do so, there would be an opposing action. Examples are Violet and Chebulic Myrobalan. The Violet and Chebulic Myrobalan act as purgatives. Violet does this with the help of its laxative property. Chebulic Myrobalan does this by pressuring on the food and making it dense. If they are made to act jointly, the action of one will nullify the action of the other. If Chebulic Myrobalan acts first and produces its squeezing effect and then Violet is given, neither will provide purgation. If the Violet acts first and produces laxity and then Chebulic Myrobalan produces squeezing, the resultant action will be very strong.

Foods such as Aloe, Gum Tragacanth and Indian Bdellium are another type of mixed foods. The Aloe produces purgation and cleanses the intestines. It also causes intestinal abrasion and opens the pores of veins. Gum Tragacanth reduces adhesiveness and produces constipation. If Gum Tragacanth and Jewish-Makkan Bdellium Resin are used along with Aloe, the former, by producing adhesion, would remove intestinal abrasion caused by aloe while the latter would restore strength to the pores of the veins and thus safety would be achieved.

WHEN THE COMBINATION OF OPPOSITE NATURAL QUALITIES IS HELPFUL OR ADVERSE TO THE NATURAL QUALITY OF THE FOOD

It is helpful when tenuousness combines with a sour taste and makes the food cooler. The adverse effect may be illustrated by another example. When a food becomes dense, its cooling capacity is reduced.

When an acrid taste combines with a taste of bitterness, it indicates that a food will be cleansing and astringent.

When there is an acrid and bitter taste, the food will be useful in treating flabbiness from wounds. It will also be useful in treating any kind of diarrhea caused by obstructions. In general, whenever an acrid and bitter taste are found together, the food will be good for the stomach and the liver. However, too much bitterness and pungency in taste indicates that the food will be harmful to the organs in the cavities of the body.

But when a taste of bitterness appears along with a biting taste, they form a useful combination. This is due to the fact that a bitter taste reflects a cleansing property while a biting taste shows the foods ability to strengthen the organs in the cavities of the body, especially those in the abdominal cavity (viscera). It is to be remembered that a biting taste along with a slightly bitter one shows that a food has a pressuring power to expel bilious humours and water. However, it also indicates that the food will not have the power to remove gluey, sticky, thick phlegm as in the case of absinthe.

All sweet tasting foods that have a tinge of a biting taste are desirable for the organs in the cavities of the body, especially those in the abdominal cavity, because these are delicious and tonic. These are also useful in dryness of the lungs because they are moderate foods.

All foods that have an acrid or biting taste because of their dryness and are also greasy or tasteless or sweet, indicate that they will resist irritation and promote the growth of flesh.

Foods that have a biting taste in addition to acridity and bitterness indicate that a food will be useful in treating wounds that are congested with pus. It will serve to increase their healing process.

These qualities are formed in accordance with their natural qualities and tastes.

When Certain Tastes Are Impure at the Beginning and with Time Become Purified

For example, the juice of sour grapes becomes pure in sour taste after a length of time due to the profuse sedimentation of acrid objects.

When Taste is Pure, Not Mixed With Another Taste, Over Time Mixes with Another Taste and Becomes Adulterated

An example is honey. If it remains for a long time, it becomes bitter and biting or such as an extract of grapes that over time become bitter and biting.

When Time Enhances a Taste

Time may enhance the bitterness and pungency of taste. For instance, the initial bitterness of grape juice is transformed into pungency with the passage of time.

ODORS

Odors are sometimes the result of heat and sometimes that of cold. It is, however, heat that passes an odor to the sense of smell. In a general sense, it is the thinning and vaporous food of the air that allows an odor to reach the sense of smell. It may also happen that the air transforms into the odor without dissolving the food creating the odor. However, the first way is more prevalent. In general it can be said that odors that cause irritation or are more inclined to be sweet are hot and odors that are sensed in sour, moldy or moist foods are cold.

In regard to perfumes, most of them are hot other than those that come from moist foods and thereby soothe the soul and the mind. Examples are Camphor and Waterlily. These foods are not lacking in coldness that accompanies the odor to the brain. All other perfumes are basically hot. The same is true for all aromatic spices, the cause behind them sometimes causing headaches.

COLORS

The natural color of a food guides us to just one particular property. Some foods of one class have a number of sub-classes that differ one from the other. Some of them tend towards being white and others to being red or black. Those that tend to be white and also have a cold temperament would be extremely cold while those that incline to red or black colors would be less cold.

It has to be noted that different foods behave differently. We have just mentioned a few that are most frequent.

BECOMING FAMILIAR WITH THE PROPERTIES OF SIMPLE FOODS

It may be stated that the simple healing foods have the following healing actions:

1. General Healing Properties: These include simple healing foods that are hot, cold, absorbing, repulsing, ulcerating, wound healing and so forth. The actions of these simple foods may be useful or harmful is general. The entire body responds to them directly.
2. Specific Healing Properties: These include simple foods that are useful in treating cancer, piles, jaundice and so forth.
3. General Healing in Appearance, but Actually Specific: These include

healing actions that may also be similar to general ones such as causing diarrhea or promoting the discharge of urine.

GENERAL HEALING PROPERTIES

Now we will discuss the general healing actions of simple foods and those that resemble them. The general healing actions are of two kinds: primary and secondary.

GENERAL HEALING PROPERTIES: PRIMARY

The primary healing properties are based on temperament. There are four types: cold, hot, moist or dry.

GENERAL HEALING PROPERTIES: SECONDARY

Secondary properties are of two types:

1 Measurable: Foods have the natural qualities of hot, cold, wet and dry. These are similar to the temperament of general healing, but they are capable of being measured as being either intense or mild. Their properties would include, for instance, burning, putrefying, congealing and maturating. These qualities of healing are the very levels of hot and cold that can be measured and compared.
2 Specific type of healing from the primary type that appear to be general contain healing properties that come from the primary type. For example, anaesthetization, scar producing, absorption, adhesiveness, opening and so forth.
3 Specific healing properties come from the above type such as anaesthetization, scar producing, absorption, adhesiveness, opening and so forth.

NATURAL PROPERTIES OF SIMPLE FOODS

We say that foods themselves have natural qualities. In addition, some properties of these foods may relate to odor or color. There are others that have contrary properties. Among these are the following eleven:

Coagulant   Light
Dehydrating   Liquid
Dense   Oily
Fragile   Thin in Consistency
Gum extract   Thick
Heavy

The properties of a coagulant food are naturally fit to move on a surface and change its position. However, due to its very cold nature, it actually retains its own form as well as its position. An example is that of wax. It appears to be naturally fluid, but it has actually coagulated.

A food that is dehydrating is one that has extensive cold and dry qualities. When it mixes with water or any other moisture, it absorbs the water or other moisture through it pores although this action remains invisible.

A dense food is one that does not break down into small parts and spread throughout the body. It remains dense. Examples are white pumpkin.

A fragile food is one that is coagulant and dry. It can break into small parts even under the slightest of pressure. An example is that of a superior quality aloe.

When gum extract is put in water or a liquid food, it breaks apart by mixing with the moistness of that food. As a result, a new thick food is formed. Examples are psyllium husk seeds and marsh mallow. Unroasted seeds having this quality may serve as a purgative because of their gluey, stickiness. When roasted, the gluey, stickiness of the seeds turns into being adhesive and astringent.

A heavy food is self-explanatory.

A light food is self-explanatory.

A liquid food is one that cannot maintain its particular form and position when it is placed on a hard food. The higher parts of it move in all possible directions. All liquids may be taken as examples. All liquid foods are opening if they are hot or moderate in temperament.

An oily food is one that contains within its food some kind of oil. An example would be some seeds.

A food that is described as being thin in consistency is because it breaks into small parts and spreads throughout our bodies. This is due to its Innate Heat in the body. Examples are saffron and cinnamon. A food having a thinning property is highly useful because of its ability to effectively dry a food. Its power to dry a food is similar to the power of a strong and irritant food, but a thinning food does not cause irritation. All tenuous foods are opening.

A thick or gluey, sticky food is a food that holds its healing properties as potential powers even when coming in contact with the Innate Heat of our body. It becomes active when it mixes with the Innate Heat of our body. If you stretch it, it remains suspended. It does not break. If both sides are stretched, it will continue to increase without breaking. An example is that of honey.

NATURAL ACTIONS OF SIMPLE HEALING FOODS BASED ON NATURAL QUALITIES

In regard to the healing properties of natural foods, we will only discuss those qualities that are well-known by nutritionists. They will be explained along with their names and forms. These relate to the four natural qualities or temperaments: twenty-two relate to a food's innately being hot; six relate to a food's innately being cold; another six relate to a food's being innately wet or moist; eight relate to a food's being innately dry; and seven relate to general properties that are either useful or harmful such as a simple natural foods being fatal, poisonous, an antidote, a purgative, a diuretic or a perspiration-producing food.

HEALING ACTIONS OF AN INNATE HOT TEMPERAMENT

Absorbing	Itch-producing
Caustic	Opening
Cauterizing	Oxidating
Cleansing	Relaxing
Corrosive	Roughening
Decay-producing	Skin-peeling
Digestive	Skin-redness producing
Diluting	Stone-dissolving
Dissolving	Ulcer-producing
Erosive	Warming
Gas-relieving	Irritating

HEALING ACTIONS OF AN INNATE COLD TEMPERAMENT

Cooling	Sleep-producing
Immature	Thickening
Repellent	Tonic

HEALING ACTIONS OF AN INNATE WET TEMPERAMENT

Gas-producing	Smoothing
Lubricant	Washing
Moistening	Wound polluting

HEALING ACTIONS OF AN INNATE DRY TEMPERAMENT

Adhesive	Flesh-producing
Astringent	Healing
Constricting	Obstruction producing
Drying	Scar producing

HEALING ACTIONS THAT MAY BE USEFUL OR HARMFUL

Antidote	Perspiration producing

GENERAL INFORMATION REGARDING THE HEALING PROPERTIES

1 Foods having a dissolving property that is also astringent are considered to be moderate foods. They are useful in treating joint ailments.
2 Whenever a food contains dissolving and astringent properties, it helps in attaining dryness.
3 In most cases, foods that combine purgative and diuretic powers each increase the power of the other. The diuretic property most often dries feces and the purgative reduces urine.
4 Foods containing both hot and cold qualities are beneficial in treating inflammatory swellings from the beginning and until the end of the swelling. This is done by means of their cold astringency and

opening or deobstruent qualities and the hot qualities it contains.

5   Foods that have the natural quality of being an antidote that are hot are more useful than other foods in treating coldness of the heart.

Above all there is a Power that distributes and provides a suitable temperament to all foods.

ALPHABETICAL DESCRIPTION OF THE PROPERTIES OF FOODS

Now we give an account of all these actions and define them.

ABSORBENT

An absorbent food (hot) is one that takes a food in and makes it part of the existing whole. It does this because of its thin consistency (tenuousness) and heat. An example is castoreum. A food is called absorbent (assimilative) because its ability to draw in foods is very effective. This type of food helps in absorbing and then expelling tiny, bony thorns and spearheads.

ADHESIVE

An adhesive (dry) food has the property of being a dry food with some moisture and thickness. It is in this way that it sticks to the openings in the body. It plugs them as well as blocks the flow of the food. It grows closer to becoming hot the more thicker, flowing and slippery it becomes. At that point, the digested food becomes more adhesive and obstruction-producing.

ANTIDOTE

An antidote (useful food) preserves the "breath," maintains its vitality and soundness enabling it to remove the harmful effect of poisons. There is no basic difference between a mineral antidote and an herbal antidote.

ASTRINGENT

An astringent (dry) food is one that creates density in the parts and the state of an organ because of its excessive movement. It also closes the meridians.

CAUSTIC

Caustic (hot) foods are foods that dissolve the humours of the organs that are thin in consistency. An ashy food is then left behind. An example is Gum Euphorbia.

CAUTERIZING

A cauterizing (hot) food is a food that dries, burns and hardens the skin. The skin then takes on the appearance of burnt coal. If there is any liquid humour present, the dried, burnt or hardened skin blocks the flow of the liquid humour and is called slough. These foods are used to prevent blood from seeping out of the veins. Examples are White or Yellow Vitriol.

CLEANSING

A cleansing food (hot) is a food that has the power to move viscous and congealed fluids from the pores of the surface of an organ and thereby remove them. An example is Honey Water. It should be noted that every cleansing food may also be a laxative even though it has no purgative power. Naturally, every bitter food is cleansing. Cleansing foods function in this way because they contain the following properties:
1   tenuous and dissolving
2   tenuous and erosive
3   tenuous and washing

CONSTRICTING

A constricting (dry) food is a food that joins the parts of the body together. Its thick moisture is put under pressure and forced to separate.

COOLING

Cooling (cold) foods are those which produce a cold temperament.

CORROSIVE

A corrosive (hot) food is a food with strong dissolving and ulcer-producing properties that severely damage flesh. An example is Verdigris.

DECAY-PRODUCING

A decay-causing (hot) food is a food that pollutes the "breath" of the temperament of an organ. It also pollutes the temperament of a fluid. As a result, the fluid ceases to be part of the organ. However, this is not done to the extent that it is burnt or corroded. It dissolves serous, phlegmatic humour (although some polluted parts remain), then acts with our body's Innate Heat to cause putrefaction. Examples are Arsenic and Wild Rue.

Digestive

A digestive (hot) food is a food which helps with food digestion.

Diluting

A diluting (hot) food is a food that greatly dilutes the humour because of its moderate heat. Examples include Hyssop, Wild Thyme and Camomile. Diluting foods function in this way because they contain the following properties:

1   tenuous and dissolving
2   tenuous and erosive
3   tenuous and washing

Dissolving

Because of the intensity of its heat, a dissolving food is capable of spreading the humour. It does this by gradually evaporating and dislodging it until its energy eliminates whatever humour is left. An example is Castoreum. Dissolving foods function in this way because they contain the following properties:

1   tenuous and dissolving
2   tenuous and erosive
3   tenuous and washing

Diuretic

Diuretic foods promote the production of urine and increase the excretion of water from the body.

Drying

A drying (dry) food eliminates fluids because of its dissolving and diluting qualities.

Erosive

Because of the thin consistency of an erosive (hot) food, it penetrates the surface of an organ. It then attaches itself to a thick humour. It separates thickness from thinness, thereby providing the parts of the humour an alternative surface. The humour can then be effectively expelled from the place that it occupies. Examples are Mustard and Oxymel. Stand ing in sharp contrast to sticky, thick foods, it is not necessary for erosive foods to affect the consistency of the humour. Instead it separates the humour into parts with each part retaining its original consistency.

FATAL

A fatal (harmful) food is a food that greatly corrupts temperament. Examples are Gum Euphorbia and Opium.

FLESH-PRODUCING

A flesh-producing (dry) food is a food that converts blood congested on the top of a wound into flesh. It does this by moderating the temperament of the blood. The temperament is thickened through drying.

GAS PRODUCING

A gas-producing (wet or moist) food creates foreign and dense humours. It does not swiftly dissolve with the action of Innate Heat. Rather, it transforms into stomach gas. Kidney beans are an example. It should be noted that gas-producing foods create headaches and are harmful for the eyes. Some of the gas-producing foods transform into gas in the first phase of digestion. This produces gas in the stomach. When it reaches the intestines, its gas-production is reduced. A food that contains unnecessary, superfluous matter also contains gas-producing food. This reaction occurs in the veins, not in the stomach and remains only partial. The remaining is completed in the veins. If the reaction of the food is to be completed in the stomach, it transforms into gas. In this case, it has no reaction in the stomach. The reaction takes place in the veins. In other words, every food that has unnecessary, extra foreign matter is gas-producing. Examples include Dried Ginger and Watercress. Also, all foods that produce gas in the veins also cause the penis to become erect, which sparks a male's sexual desire.

GAS-RELIEVING

A gas-relieving (hot) food is a food that through its hot and drying properties dilutes the consistency of the gas by giving it a more gaseous nature. The gas is thus dissolved and removed. An example is Common Rue Seeds.

HEALING

A healing food (dry) has the property of drying and thickening the fluid collected between the two layers of a wound. It does this so that the fluid becomes adhesive and thick. Both ends of the wound attach them-selves to each other, for example, Aloe.

IMMATURE

An immature (cold) food has properties that are the opposite of di-gestive and maturating foods. Due to its cold nature, it causes extraneous heat on food and humours to be ineffective. Food is then is left undigested and humors, immature.

IRRITANT

An irritant (hot) food is a food that is so penetrating and thin in consistency (tenuous) that it splits a compact food into numerous parts, each part being similar in shape, but different in quantity. These parts are so small that they are not perceptible individually, but only when taken as a whole. Examples are a Poultice of Mustard with Vinegar or Vinegar alone.

ITCH-PRODUCING

Because of its intense heat and absorption properties, itch-produc-ing (hot) foods cause the irritating, itching matter to move to the pores, but it does not ulcerate. An example is Wild Celery.

LUBRICATING

A lubricating (wet or moist) food causes whatever is within the body that has the ability to flow, to flow when the food reaches the surface of the body. Through its repulsive power, it softens and pushes it out of its place. An example is the Plum in treating cases of diarrhea.

MINERAL ANTIDOTE

A mineral antidote (useful food) preserves the "breath" while it maintains its vitality. Its vitality and soundness enables it to remove the harmful effect of poisons. It should be noted that there is no basic difference between a mineral antidote and an herbal antidote.

MOISTENING

Foods that produce wetness and moisture in the body.

OBSTRUCTION-PRODUCING

Due to its dense, dry or adhesive properties, an obstruction-pro-ducing (dry) food is retained in the orifices of the body where obstructions are produced.

OPENING

An opening (hot) food disturbs matter lying deep in the cavity or orifice. It then opens the passages. Foods with an opening property are stronger than cleansing foods. Opening foods function in this way because they contain the following properties:

1   tenuous and dissolving
2   tenuous and erosive
3   tenuous and washing

OXIDATING

An oxidating (hot) food maturates the humour. It does this through its possibility of its astringent properties. Rather than rapidly dissolving it, it holds onto the humour until it is ripe. It divides fluidity from dryness. This process is called "blood oxidization."

PERSPIRATION

Perspiration-producing foods open the pores of the skin, which causes a person to sweat.

POISONOUS

A poisonous (harmful) food corrupts the temperament. This is due to its inherent specific property. An example is Aconite.

PURGATIVE

Purgative foods are well-known. It should be noted that every food that is a purgative is also astringent. An example is Hermodactyle. This herb is very useful in treating rheumatism. This is because the purgative power of the food absorbs foods while its astringent abilities help in the passage of foods. Thus foods do not move towards joints nor do they replace any other food.

RELAXANT

A relaxant (hot) food is a food that softens the texture of organs that have dense pores. Because of its heat and fluidity, the pores become wider. It helps with the expulsion of unnecessary, superfluous matter deposited there. Examples are a Poultice with Dill and Linseed.

REPELLENT

A repellent (cold) food is the opposite of an absorbent food. This is because of its inherent cold nature in addition to some cooling effect in an organ. Its cooling effect causes it to be dense. It narrows down pores. It breaks its absorbing heat. It condenses fluid that flows towards it or it coagulates it. In this way, it prevents it from reaching an organ. Examples are Garden Nightshade used in cases of swellings.

ROUGHENING

A roughening (hot) food causes the surface of an organ to become uneven because of the great amount of its astringency. Its astringency is combined with either its density or the intensity of its pungency as well as its thinning ability. It may also cleanse a rough surface that had been smooth. The thick fluid flows over it when the rough or uneven surface of a dense organ is cleansed. It is replaced with a new, smooth surface removing the original roughness. An example is Sweet Melilot. This takes place for the most part in bones and cartilages. It rarely affects the skin. Roughening foods function in this way because they contain the following properties:

1   tenuous and astringent
2   tenuous and very pungent
3   tenuous and washing

SCAR-PRODUCING

Drying up the surface of a wound and forming dead skin are the properties of a scar-producing food. While the natural skin is regenerating, this dead skin provides protection against injury. All foods that are moderately hot or cold-tempered are drying without causing irritation.

SKIN PEELER

A skin-peeler (hot) is a food that cleans parts of decayed skin because of its intense cleansing property. Examples are Costus, Rhubarb and all other foods that are useful in treating skin rashes and freckles.

SKIN-REDNESS PRODUCING

A skin-redness producing (hot) food is a food that warms an organ so intensely that blood is attracted towards the organ. The result is that the skin appears red on the outside. Examples include Mustard, Figs, Mountain Mint and Caraway. The effect of the skin-redness producing food is nearly the same as that of cauterization.

SLEEP-PRODUCING

A sleep-inducing food (cold) is a food that cools the whole body. It dissolves the "breath" of an organ with its coldness to the point that motor and sensory powers take on a cold temperament, causing matter to become dense. It de-sensitizes the temperament of the organ so much so that it does not respond to the psychic powers. Examples include Opium and Henbane.

SMOOTHING

A smoothing (wet or moist) food is a thick food that spreads over the surface of a dry organ and smooths it, causing the external surface of that body to become smooth. Dryness is concealed beneath some fluid that flows and spreads over it.

STONE-DISSOLVING

A stone-dissolving (hot) food heals stone-like matter. It reduces it to minute pieces and crushes it. An example is Wild Rue.

THICKENING

A thickening (cold) food is the opposite of a diluting food. A thickening food causes a fluid to become dense. It does this through its property of condensing or coagulating.

TONIC

A tonic (cold) food moderates an organ's temperament. It does this to the point that an organ itself resists the superfluous matter moving towards it. This tonic property comes from either its inherent property, as with sealing clay and antidotes, or through its moderate temperament that causes what is hot-tempered to become cold-tempered and vice versa. Galen explained the action of Rose Oil in this way.

ULCER-PRODUCING

An ulcer-producing (hot) is a food that destroys and dissolves the serous humours formed in the structure of skin. An ulcer is caused when it attracts the injurious matter. An example is the Marking Nut.

WASHING

Because of its moisture, a washing (wet or moist) food has a passive cleansing power. This becomes active when in contact with another food.

This contact is made either through motion or flow. A washing food first softens whenever a thin consistency matter flows to the opening of the veins. It subsequently washes away this softened matter. Examples are Barley Water and Pure Water.

WARMING

A warming (hot) food are those which produce warmth to our temperament.

WOUND-POLLUTING

A wound-producing food (wet or moist) when applied, causes the secretions of a wound to increase. In this way it prevents wound from drying and healing.

RULES AND EXAMPLES FOR DETERMINING THE NATURE AND USES OF FOODS

Sometimes foods are cooked, ground, burned, washed or frozen or placed near some other food. There are foods that lose their properties from any of these processes. It may be that one food is mixed with another food. The following, then, applies:

COOKING FOODS

With some foods, their density is so much that even cooking them does not permit their healing properties to operate. This is the case unless cooking is extremely hard. Examples are the root of caper, Indian Birthwort and Long Zedoary.

With other foods, their temperament is so excessive that only a moderate amount of cooking is necessary for their healing properties to work. In this case, if they are cooked hard, their properties will disappear. Examples are Diuretic Seeds, Lavender and similar other foods.

Then there are foods that need only a light cooking. Hard cooking causes them to lose their properties to the extent that what remains is no longer useful. An example is Epithyme. Just cooking it fairly well causes it to lose its properties.

Grinding Foods

Grinding foods may cause them to loose their healing properties. An example is scammony. As a result, it should only be ground lightly. This allows the heat generated not to destroy its actions. This is true of most gums. It is better to dissolve them in fluids rather than to grind them.

If foods are ground excessively, they lose their inherent, healing properties. This is the case with all foods. When a food is broken into pieces, the pieces do not necessarily maintain their intrinsic properties. This is dependent upon the proportion of volume to the whole food. It could also be that the potency of a food decreases to such an extent that it is no longer capable of performing its natural functions.

Excessively ground foods that have some specific properties may take on a different property. For example, a food that is capable of evacuating a humour or other superfluous matter may lose this ability to do this. Due to the loss of its original property, it may evacuate only the serous humour. These foods, because of their minute size, are more penetrating, reaching an organ rapidly even though this was not previously possible. It happens particularly when there is an abundant quantity. Therefore, it is necessary that foods that are by constitution thin in consistency should not be ground excessively. On the other hand, foods that are dense and slow in movement should be ground completely so that they are able to penetrate to remotest parts of the body. Such medicines are used for lung diseases. Examples are coral, pearl, hematite and so forth.

Burning Foods

In some cases, it is useful to burn foods in order to reduce or to increase their usefulness. Pungent, thinning and moderate foods, reduce their pungency as well as their heat when they are burnt. This occurs because the burning dissolves the inherent hot and dry quality of the food.

There is an increase of intensity when foods that are dense and neither hot nor intense in their potency are burnt. An example is Lime. It is a stone, but when burnt it takes on intensity.

There are five reasons for burning foods: (1) to reduce their intensity; (2) to increase their potency; (3) to dilute their dense food; (4) to prepare them for grinding; (5) and to eliminate corrupt foods.

WASHING FOODS

Washing a food causes it to lose its intense and delicate property. It causes it to become a soothing medicine. It cools down its intense heat in some cases. Where hot and dry properties are produced from burning, washing removes those properties from all those cold and dry foods.

Cooling down the heat of a food is the main purpose for washing it. Washing causes a food to break into small pieces. It becomes completely cleansed in this way.

CONGEALING FOODS

Congealing foods renders the thinning property of all foods to become ineffective. Foods that are already cold-tempered increase in coldness.

STORING AND COLLECTING SIMPLE FOODS

STORAGE OF FOODS

Storing foods near other foods may cause either of them or both of them to produce new properties. In this way, their inherent healing property changes. Many cold foods can become hot-tempered when kept with hot-tempered ingredients. Many hot foods can become cold-tempered when stored with cold-tempered ingredients. This is an important point to remember. One should not keep different tempered types of foods near one another.

COLLECTING FOODS

- Foods used should be fresh. This is absolutely necessary. Nuts should not be shriveled or broken prior to consumption. The best nuts are those that have reached their full weight.
- Foods collected when the weather is clear are better than those that collected when there is humid or rainy weather.
- Wild growing foods are stronger than cultivated foods. Wild growing foods are usually smaller in size.
- Foods that grow on hills or on mountain sides are stronger than foods that grow on the plains.

- Foods collected from forests and places that are exposed to the sun's rays are better than those gathered from shady places.
- Clearly, foods collected at the right time are better than those collected at the wrong time.

Note that the strength of herbs is weakened after three years. However, this does not apply to other foods. Examples are black and white hellebore that maintain their strength longer. Foods are of mineral, vegetable and of animal origin.

MINERAL FOODS

Among the mineral foods, the best are those that are extracted from well-known mines. It is essential that the food selected has its specific physical structure maintaining its characteristic taste and color.

VEGETABLE AND HERBAL FOODS

Vegetable and herbal foods consist of leaves, roots, seeds, branches, flowers, fruits, gums and all other plant parts. Leaves should be gathered when they have reached their full size, having maintained their form, color and potency. In addition, leaves that have fallen or are scattered should not be used.

Roots: Roots should be gathered when their trees or plants have shed their leaves. Roots should not be deformed or crooked.

Seeds: Seeds should be taken when they have condensed and their moisture is disappeared. Seeds should have been formed within their fruit. Seeds should be mature and untraveled.

Branches: Branches should be taken when they have reached perfection before they have begun drying.

Flowers: Flowers should be gathered when they have reached their full bloom. However, they should not be dried up or fallen from the tree or plant.

Fruits: It is essential that fruits be gathered when they have fully matured, but before they fall from the tree or plant. The best fruit are those that have attained full size and weight.

Gums: Gums should be collected when they have coagulated. However, they should not have grown to such extent that they begin to lose their properties. Most of the gums lose their strength after three years. This is particularly the case with euphoria. Its potency depends on its excellence. If it is difficult to collect a fresh food of full strength, the older and the weaker one may be taken in twice the amount of the fresh food, regardless of its class.

These are the general principles that Avicenna explains in his introduction to Volume 2 of the *Canon of Medicine* in regards to simple foods.

***

This marks the end of our journey through the Avicenna Cuisine Guidebook, an art that had been lost for centuries with only rootless vestiges of it remaining, while keeping in mind that the adventure of cooking with Avicenna Cuisine is just beginning. We have explored the theories of the Seven Nature-Given Essentials, the Six Nurturing Essentials, Dietetics, Determining Your Temperament and, then, for the first time in 1000 years in the English language, learning exactly how to determine the temperament of the foods we eat. We are now able to focus our diets on healthy choices that will balance our humours and, therefore, our temperaments for a harmonious body, mind and spirit.

It has been written with the hope that we can further the research in finding the temperaments of foods to develop and expand our Avicenna Cuisine database of ingredients.

For more information, please visit www.avicennacuisine.com.

Share your cultural experience and story if you have
heard about this renowned hot, cold, wet and dry system.

Facebook.com/AvicennaCuisine
Twitter.com/AvicennaCuisine
#AvicennaCuisine

Endnotes to the Text

1. See Avicenna, the *Canon of Medicine* Volume 1: *General Medicine,* Chicago: Kazi Publications, 1999. Notes by Gruner p 569. All text from the *Canon of Medicine* is with the permission of the copyright holder. This permission includes excerpts from pp 131 ff; p. 31 ff; pp 17-18; pp 143 ff; pp 24-25; p 219 ff; pp 188 ff; p 215; pp 146-147; pp 224; pp 411 ff; p 40; pp 275 ff; pp 435-437 ff; and p 239. The *Canon of Medicine* Volume 2: *Natural Pharmaceuticals*, Chicago: Kazi Publications, 2011, Avicenna's Introduction. The *Canon of Medicine* Volume 3: *Special Pathologies*, pp 569-597.

2. "The Four Temperaments" by Rev. Conrad Hock, revised and enlarged by Rev. Nicholas M. Wilwers, S.A.C.; M.A.; S.T.B; Nihil Obstat: H. B. Ries, Censor Liborum; Imprimi Potest: Otto Boenki, S.A.C. Superior Maior. With the permission of Father Bill Lemanski of the Pallottine Fathers, Milwaukee, WI who said about the essay: A short but valuable knowledge with practical suggestions is supplied by Conrad Hock, "The Four Temperaments." Having been out of print for some years it is now herewith revised, enlarged and offered to the public. The texts on temperament, unless otherwise indicated, are from The Pallottine Fathers, Milwaukee. With the permission of Father Bill Lemanski.

3. *Encyclopaedia Britannica*, 1974: (15th edition) 1974;3:846

4. Sina, 2010: Sina I. *Al-Qanoon Fil Tibb*. 1. Daryaganj New Delhi -2,India: Aijaz publishing house; 2010

5. Jordan Aumann, O.P. was a native of the United States and Director of the Institute of Spirituality at the Pontifical University of St. Thomas Aquinas in Rome. He was also a Consultor for the Sacred Congregation for the Clergy and Catechetics and likewise a Consultor for the Sacred Congregation for Evangelization. From 1977 onwards he had been giving special courses in spirituality at the Faculty of Theology of the University of Santo Tomas, Manila. See   https://archive.org/stream/SpiritualTheologyByFr.JordanAumannO.p/AumannO.p.SpiritualTheologyall_djvu.txt

6. The Jerrahi Sufi Order of Canada, www.jerrahi.ca/

7. See http://www.passionsandtempers.com/v1/page.php?l=en&p=humours

8. See Karima Burns, http://www.onislam.net/english/health-and-science/health/441948-the-physical-characteristics-of-temperament.html.

9. See http://www.fsspminneapolis.org/temperamental-discourses/

10. See http://www.sufiorder.toronto.on.ca/purification_breaths.htm

11. See Karima Burns, http://www.onislam.net/english/health-and-science/health/441948-the-physical-characteristics-of-temperament.html

12. See *Why You Act the Way You Do* by Tim LaHaye, Tyndale House Publishers, Inc., 2012

13. See http://www.fsspminneapolis.org/temperamental-discourses/

14. See the Jerrahi Sufi Order of Canada' www.jerrahi.ca/ (Fiery Element)

15. See http://www.passionsandtempers.com/v1/page.php?l=en&p=humours

16. See Jordan Aumann, https://archive.org/stream/SpiritualTheology-ByFr.JordanAumannO.p/AumannO.p.SpiritualTheologyall_djvu.txt. With the permission of Father Bill Lemanski of the Pallottines Fathers.

17. *ibid.*

18. See http://www.sufiorder.toronto.on.ca/purification_breaths.htm

19. See Karima Burns, http://www.onislam.net/english/health-and-science/health/441948-the-physical-characteristics-of-temperament.html)

20. *op. cit,* Jordan Aumann.

21. See http://www.fsspminneapolis.org/temperamental-discourses/

22. http://www.sufiorder.toronto.on.ca.htm

23. See http://www.passionsandtempers.com/v1/page.php?l=en&p=humours

24. Hakim G. M. Chishti N.D., *Traditional Healer's Handbook*, Healing Arts Press, 1988.

25. See Jordan Aumann, *op. cit.*

26. See http://www.sufiorder.toronto.on.ca/purification_breaths.htm

27. http://www.huuu.org/learn/elements-attributes.html

28. See http://www.fsspminneapolis.org/temperamental-discourses/

29. http://www.sufiorder.toronto.on.ca.htm

30. See http://www.passionsandtempers.com/v1/page.php?l=en&p=humours

31. http://www.huuu.org/learn/elements-attributes.html

32. See http://www.sufiorder.toronto.on.ca.htm

33. See http://www.sufiorder.toronto.on.ca/purification_breaths.htm

34. See http://www.huuu.org/learn/elements-attributes.html

35. http://www.huuu.org/learn/elements-attributes.html

36. See http://www.fsspminneapolis.org/temperamental-discourses/

37. The difference between digestion and putrefaction is that in the case of digestion, the heat and moisture that are present in matter are altered; that is, instead of being accordant with the original temperament, they are now accordant with another one. In oxidation, moist substances are separated from dry ones by sublimation and evaporation, where the dryness goes into the residue. In the process of simple heating, the humours

simply become warmer without losing their natural breath.

38. Nicholas Culpeper (18 October 1616 – 10 January 1654) was an English botanist, herbalist, physician, and astrologer. His published books include *The English Physician* (1652) and the *Complete Herbal* (1653), which contain a rich store of pharmaceutical and herbal knowledge, and *Astrological Judgement of Diseases from the Decumbiture of the Sick* (1655), which is one of the most detailed documents we have on the practice of medical astrology in Early Modern Europe.
59. See *ibid.*

39. See *ibid.*

40. See *ibid.*

41. See *ibid.*

42. See *ibid.*

43. William Salmon (1644–1713) was English empiric doctor, advertising himself as "Professor of Physick", and a writer of medical texts. *The Practice of Physick,* 1709. See

http://bearmedicineherbals.com/greek-herbal-medicine-the-four-qualities-and-the-four-degrees-by-matthew-wood.html

44. See Culpeper, *op. cit.*

45. See *op. cit.,* Salmon.

APPENDIX: DETAIL OF CONTENTS PAGES

Part III. Dietetics
CHAPTER 14
On Digestion and Related Matters • 53

CHAPTER 19
Fiery Temperament
Humour: Yellow Bile
Basic Qualities: Hot and Dry • 105

CHAPTER 20
Earthy Temperament
Humour: Black Bile

CHAPTER 21
Watery Temperament
Humour: Phlegm

Basic Qualities: Cold and Wet • 135